Automating and Testing a REST API

A Case Study in API testing using: Java, REST Assured,
Postman, Tracks, cURL and HTTP Proxies

Alan Richardson

Automating and Testing a REST API

A Case Study in API testing using: Java, REST Assured, Postman, Tracks, cURL and HTTP Proxies

Alan Richardson

ISBN 978-0-9567332-9-0

First published in Great Britain in 2017 by Compendium Developments Ltd (http://www.compendiumdev.co.uk)

contact details: alan@compendiumdev.co.uk

e-book ISBN : 978-0-9567332-8-3

paper book ISBN : 978-0-9567332-9-0

Contents

Introduction

We can read on-line about the "Test Automation Pyramid" and we can also learn that "GUI Automation is brittle" and "we should test under the GUI". Fine. But how many in-depth examples can you find? Examples that show you how to automate quickly, and how to improve on that initial 'quick fix'?

That's what this case study is all about - an example of automating an application without using GUI based libraries.

This case study will show how you can add value to a process quickly with fairly crude and "hacky" code, and then how you can change that code to make it better.

Throughout the case study, I'm not just going to tell you how I did it. I'm going to explain why, and what I could have done differently. Why I made the decisions I made, because then you can try different approaches and build on this case study.

Since this is a case study, and not a 'step by step' course. I assume some basic knowledge:

- You know how to install Java and an IDE,
    - if you don't then the Starter Page[1] on Java For Testers will help.
- You have some basic Web experience or HTTP knowledge,
    - if not then my Technical Web Testing 101[2] course might help or my YouTube channel[3].

I'll cover some of the above topics, although not in depth. If you get stuck you can use the resources above or contact me[4].

The background behind this case study is that I've used Tracks as an Application Under Test in a few workshops, for practising my own testing, and to improve my ability to automate.

For the workshops I built code to create users and populate the environment with test data. I found that people like to learn how to do that, and I realised during the workshops that I also approach this differently to other people.

---

[1]http://javafortesters.com/page/install/

[2]http://compendiumdev.co.uk/page.php?title=techweb101course

[3]http://eviltester.com/youtube

[4]http://compendiumdev.co.uk/contact

I didn't automate under the GUI because I follow a "Test Automation Pyramid". I automated beneath the GUI:

- because it is fast,
- because we can do things we can't do through the GUI.

By 'Under the GUI' I mean:

- Using the API (Application Programming Interface).
- Using the 'APP as API',
    - sending through the HTTP that the GUI would have sent, but not using the GUI.

I explain 'App as API' in the case study later, and show examples of it in practice. I realised, during the teaching of this stuff, that most people don't automate in this way.

For most people testing 'under the GUI' means API. To me it means working at the different system communication points anywhere 'under' the GUI. I explain this in the case study as well.

Working under the GUI isn't always easier. In this case study you'll see that working through the GUI would have been 'easier'. I wouldn't have had to manage cookie sessions and scrape data off pages.

But working beneath the GUI is faster, once it is working, and arguably is more robust - but we'll consider that in more detail in the case study and you'll see when it isn't.

You'll see initial code that I used for Tracks 2.2 and then updated for 2.3, I'll walk you through the reasons for the changes and show you the investigation process that I used and changes I made.

If you haven't automated an HTTP application below the GUI before then I think this case study will help you learn a lot, and you'll finish with a stack of ideas to take forward.

If you have automated the GUI before. I think you'll enjoy learning why I made the decisions I made, and you'll be able to compare them with the decisions you've made in the past. I think, after finishing the case study, you might expand the range of decisions you have open to you in the future.

Introduction to APIs

This chapter will provide an introduction to the concept of an API (Application Programming Interface) and concentrates on Web or Internet accessible APIs. I will explain most of the concepts that you need to understand this book and I will start from the very basics. Most of this chapter will be written colloquially for common sense understanding rather than to provide formal computer science definitions.

You can probably skip this chapter if you are familiar with Web Services, URI and URL, HTTP, HTTP Status Codes, JSON and XML.

Also, because this chapter covers a lot of definition, feel free to skip it if you want to get stuck in to the practical aspects. You can always come back to this chapter later if you don't understand some basic terminology.

First I'll start by saying that we are going to learn how to test Web Applications. i.e. Applications that you can access over a network or the internet without installing them on your machine.

The Web Application we will test has an API, which is a way of accessing the application without using a Web Browser or the application's Graphical User Interface (GUI).

What Is a Web Application?

A Web Application is a software application that is deployed to a Web Server. This means the application is installed onto a computer and users access the application via a Web Browser.

Google Is an Example of a Web Application

google.com is an example of a Web Application. A user visits google.com in a Browser and the application's Graphical User Interface (GUI) is displayed in the Browser. The GUI consists of a search input field which the user fills in and then clicks a button to search the Web.

When the user clicks the search button, the Browser makes a request to the Web Application on the Web Server to have the Google Search Application make the search and return the results to the user in the form of a web page with clickable links.

Basically,

- Web Browser -> Sends a Request to -> Web Application
- Web Application -> Processes Request and Sends a Web Page as Response to -> Web Browser

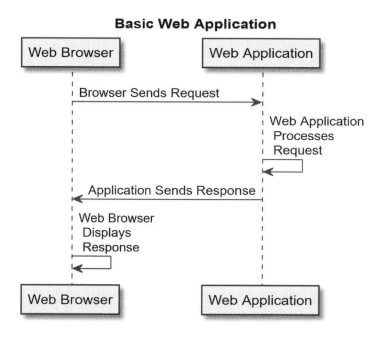

The requests that the Browser sends to the Web Server are HTTP requests. HTTP requests are a way of sending messages between machines over the Internet. Think of HTTP as the format of the message that Browser and Web Server send to each other.

When we first visit Google in a Browser we type in the URL or address for Google. i.e. `https://google.com`

The Browser then sends a type of HTTP request to Google called a `GET` request to 'get', or retrieve, the main search form. Google Web Application receives the request and replies with an HTTP response containing the HTML of the search page. HTML is the specification for the Web Page so the Browser knows how to display it to the user.

When the user types in a search term and presses the search button. The Browser sends a `POST` request to Google. The `POST` request is different from the `GET` request because it contains the details of the search term that the user wants the Google Web Application to search for.

The Google Web Application then responds with an HTTP response that contains the HTML containing all the search results matching the User's search term.

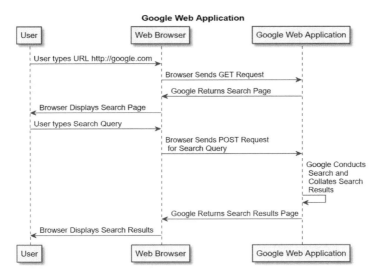

Google is an example of a Web Application with a GUI, and because the user accesses the Web Application through a Browser they are often unaware of the HTTP requests, or that different types of HTTP requests are being made.

When we test HTTP APIs we have to understand the details of HTTP requests.

What Is an API?

An API is an Application Programming Interface. This is an interface to an application designed for other computer systems to use. As opposed to a Graphical User Interface (GUI) which is designed for humans to use.

APIs come in many different forms with and technical implementations but this book concentrates on HTTP or Web APIs.

An HTTP based API is often called a Web API since they are used to access Web Applications which are deployed to Servers accessible over the Internet.

Applications which are accessed via HTTP APIs are often called Web Services.

Mobile Applications often use Web Services and REST APIs to communicate with servers to implement their functionality. The Mobile Application processes the message returned from the Web Service and displays it to the User in the application GUI. So again, the user is unaware that HTTP requests are being made, or of the format of the requests and responses.

What Is an HTTP Request?

HTTP stands for Hypertext Transfer Protocol and is a way of sending messages to software on another computer over the Internet or over a Network.

An HTTP request is sent to a specific URL and consists of:

- a VERB specifying the type of request e.g. GET, POST, PUT, DELETE
- A set of HTTP Headers. The headers specify information such as the type of Browser, type of content in the message, and what type of response is accepted in return.
- A body, or payload in the request, representing the information sent to, or from, the Web Application. Not all HTTP messages can have payloads: POST and PUT can have payloads, GET and DELETE can not.

HTTP requests are text based messages and over the course of this Case Study you will learn to read them e.g.

```
GET http://compendiumdev.co.uk/apps/mocktracks/projectsjson.php HTTP/1.1
Host: compendiumdev.co.uk
User-Agent: Mozilla/5.0 (Windows NT 10.0; Win64; x64)
 AppleWebKit/537.36 (KHTML, like Gecko)
 Chrome/59.0.3071.115 Safari/537.36
Accept: text/html,application/xhtml+xml,
 application/xml;q=0.9,image/webp,image/apng,*/*;q=0.8
```

The above HTTP request is a GET request, which is a READ request:

- to read the page from the URL
    - `http://compendiumdev.co.uk/apps/mocktracks/projectsjson.php`
- request is made from the Chrome Browser version 59. You can see this in the 'User-Agent' header. Yes, the header also mentions 'Safari', 'AppleWebKit' and 'Mozilla', this is for various reasons of backwards compatibility, but it was sent from Chrome version 59. For more information on User-Agent visit useragentstring.com[5].

---

[5]http://www.useragentstring.com

What Is a URL?

URL is a Uniform Resource Locator and is the address we use to access websites and web applications.

When working with APIs you will often see this referred to as a URI (Uniform Resource Identifier).

Think of a URI as the generic name for a URL.

When we want to call an HTTP API we need the URL for the `endpoint` we want to call e.g

`http://compendiumdev.co.uk/apps/mocktracks/projectsjson.php`

This is the locator that says "I want to call the `apps/mocktracks/projectsjson.php` resource located at `compendiumdev.co.uk` using the `http` protocol".

For the purposes of this book I will use the phrase URL, but you might see URI mentioned in some of the source code. I use URL because the locator contains the protocol or *scheme* required to access it (`http`).

The above URL can be broken down into the form:

`scheme://host/resource`

- scheme - `http`
- host - `compendiumdev.co.uk`
- resource - `apps/mocktracks/projectsjson.php`

A larger form for a URL is:

`scheme://host:port/resource?query#fragment`

I didn't use a `port` in the URL, for some applications you might need to.

By default `http` uses port 80, so I could have used:

`http://compendiumdev.co.uk:80/apps/mocktracks/projectsjson.php`

Also I haven't used a query because this endpoint doesn't need one.

The `query` is a way of passing parameters in the URL to the endpoint e.g. Google uses query parameters to define the search term and the page:

`https://www.google.co.uk/?q=test&start=10#q=test`

- scheme - `https`
- host - `www.google.co.uk`
- query - `q=test&start=10`
- fragment - `q=test`

The query is the set of parameters which are key, value pairs delimited by '&' e.g. `q=test` and `start=10` ("start" is a key, and "10" is the value for that key).

When working with APIs it is mainly the scheme, host, port and query that you will use.

You can learn more about URL and URI online[6].

What Are HTTP Verbs?

A Web Browser will usually make `GET` requests and `POST` requests.

- `GET` requests ask to read information from the server e.g. clicking on a link.
- `POST` requests supply information to the server e.g. submitting a form.

`GET` requests do not have a body, and just consist of the Verb, URL and the Headers.

`POST` requests can have a payload body e.g.

```
POST http://www.compendiumdev.co.uk/apps/mocktracks/reflect.php HTTP/1.1
Host: www.compendiumdev.co.uk
User-Agent: Mozilla/5.0 (Windows NT 10.0; Win64; x64)
 AppleWebKit/537.36 (KHTML, like Gecko)
 Chrome/59.0.3071.115 Safari/537.36
Accept: text/html,application/xhtml+xml,
 application/xml;q=0.9,image/webp,image/apng,*/*;q=0.8

{"action":"post"}
```

When working with a Web Application or HTTP API the typical HTTP Verbs used are:

- GET, to read information.

---

[6]https://en.wikipedia.org/wiki/Uniform_Resource_Identifier

- POST, to create information.
- PUT, to amend or create information.
- DELETE, to delete information, this is rarely used for Browser accessed applications, but often used for HTTP APIs.

POST and PUT requests would usually have a message body. GET and DELETE would not.

HTTP Verbs are described in the W3c Standard[7] and IETF standard[8].

What Is an HTTP Response?

When you issue an HTTP Request to the server you receive an HTTP Response.

The response from the server tells you if your request was successful, or if there was a problem.

```
HTTP/1.1 200 OK
Date: Fri, 30 Jun 2017 13:50:11 GMT
Connection: close
Content-Type: application/json

{
  "projects": {
    "project": [
      {
        "id":  1,
        "name": "A New Project",
        "position": 0,
        "description": "",
        "state": "active",
        "created-at": "2017-06-27T12:25:26+01:00",
        "updated-at": "2017-06-27T12:25:26+01:00"
      }
    ]
  }
}
```

The above response has:

---

[7]https://www.w3.org/Protocols/rfc2616/rfc2616-sec9.html
[8]https://tools.ietf.org/html/rfc7231

- A status code of 200, which means that the request was successful.
- A Content-Type header of application/json which means that the body is a JSON response.
- A body which contains the actual payload response from the server.

What Is an HTTP Status Code?

Web Services and HTTP APIs use HTTP Status Codes to tell us what happened when the server processed the request.

The simple grouping for HTTP Status Codes is:

- 1xx - Informational
- 2xx - Success e.g. 200 Success
- 3xx - Redirection e.g. 302 Temporary Redirect
- 4xx - Client Error e.g. 400 Bad Request, 404 Not Found
- 5xx - Server Error e.g. 500 Internal Server Error

The type of status code you receive depends on the application you are interacting with. Usually a 4xx error means that you have done something wrong and a 5xx error means that something has gone wrong with the application server you are interacting with.

You can learn more about status codes online:

- Wikipedia List[9]
- HTTP Statuses[10]

What Are Payloads?

A Payload is the body of the HTTP request or response.

When browsing the Web, the Browser usually receives an HTML[11] payload. This is the web page that you see rendered in the Browser.

Typically when working with an HTTP API we will send and receive JSON or XML payloads.

You saw JSON payloads in the examples above.

---

[9]https://en.wikipedia.org/wiki/List_of_HTTP_status_codes
[10]https://httpstatuses.com/
[11]https://en.wikipedia.org/wiki/HTML

What Is JSON?

JSON stands for JavaScript Object Notation and is a text representation that is also valid JavaScript code.

```
{
  "projects": {
    "project": [
      {
        "id":  1,
        "name": "A New Projectaniheeiadtatd",
        "position": 0,
        "description": "",
        "state": "active",
        "created-at": "2017-06-27T12:25:26+01:00",
        "updated-at": "2017-06-27T12:25:26+01:00"
      }
    ]
  }
}
```

JSON can be thought of as a hierarchical set of key/value pairs where the value can be:

- Object - delimited by { and }.
- Array - delimited by [and].
- String - delimited by " and ".
- Integer

An array is a list of objects or key/value pairs.

The keys are String values e.g. "projects", "project", "id", etc.

What Is XML?

XML stands for Extensible Markup Language.

HTML is a variant of XML.

```
<?xml version="1.0" encoding="UTF-8"?>
<projects type="array">
  <project>
      <id type="integer">1</id>
      <name>A New Projectaniheeiadtatd</name>
      <position type="integer">0</position>
      <description nil="true"/>
      <state>active</state>
      <created-at type="dateTime">2017-06-27T12:25:26+01:00
          </created-at>
      <updated-at type="dateTime">2017-06-27T12:25:26+01:00
          </updated-at>
      <default-context-id type="integer" nil="true"/>
      <completed-at type="dateTime" nil="true"/>
      <default-tags nil="true"/>
      <last-reviewed type="dateTime" nil="true"/>
  </project>
</projects>
```

XML is constructed from nested elements

- An element has an opening and closing tag e.g. `<state>` and `</state>`.
    - The tag has a name i.e. `state`.
    - The opening tag begins with `<` and ends with `>` e.g. `<state>`.
    - The closing tag begins with `</` and ends with `>` e.g. `</state>`.
- An element has a value, which is the text between the tags e.g. the `state` element has a value of `active`.
- An element can have attributes, these are always within the opening tag e.g. the `id` element (`<id type="integer">`) has an attribute named `type` with a value of `"integer"`.
- Elements can contain other Elements. These are called Nested Elements. e.g. the `projects` element has a nested element called `project`.

For XML to be valid, it must be well formed, meaning that every opening tag must have a corresponding closing tag, and strings must have an opening and closing quote.

Some elements do not have a closing tag, these are self closing. The opening tag, instead of ending with `>` actually ends with `/>` you can see this in the `<description nil="true"/>` element.

What Are HTTP Headers?

HTTP messages have the Verb and URL, followed by a set of headers, and then the optional payload.

```
POST http://www.compendiumdev.co.uk/apps/mocktracks/reflect.php HTTP/1.1
Host: www.compendiumdev.co.uk
Content-Type: application/json
Accept: application/json

{"action":"post"}
```

The headers are a set of meta data for the message.

Headers are a name, followed by `:`, followed by the value of the header.

The above HTTP message example has three headers:

- Host
- Content-Type
- Accept

The Host header defines the destination server domain name.

The Content-Type header tells the server that the content of this message is JSON.

The Accept header tells the server that the client (application sending the message) will only accept response payloads represented in JSON.

There are many headers available[12] for configuring the Authentication details, length of message, custom meta data, cookies etc.

What Is Authentication?

When we send a message to a server we might need to be authenticated i.e. authorised to send a message and receive a response.

For many Web Applications you authenticate yourself in the application by logging in with a username and password. The same is true for Web Services or HTTP APIs.

---

[12]https://en.wikipedia.org/wiki/List_of_HTTP_header_fields

If you are not authenticated and try to send a message to a server then you are likely to receive a response from the server with a 4xx status code e.g.

- 401 Unauthorized
- 403 Forbidden

There are many ways to authenticate HTTP requests for HTTP APIs.

Some common approaches you might encounter are:

- Custom Headers
- Basic Authentication Headers
- Session Cookies

Some HTTP APIs require **Custom Headers** e.g.

```
POST http://www.compendiumdev.co.uk/apps/mocktracks/reflect.php HTTP/1.1
X-APPLICATION_KEY: asds-234j-werw
```

Here the `X-APPLICATION-KEY` header has a secret value which authenticates the request.

Basic Authentication Headers are a standard approach for simple login details:

```
POST http://www.compendiumdev.co.uk/apps/mocktracks/reflect.php HTTP/1.1
Authorization: Basic Ym9iOmRvYmJz
```

The `Authorization` header specifies `Basic` authentication and is followed by a base64[13] encoded string.

- "`Ym9iOmRvYmJz`" is the base64 encoded version of the string "`bob:dobbs`"
- In Basic Authentication the string represents `username:password`

Session Cookies[14] are set by a server in a response message and are represented in a `Cookies:` header.

---

[13]https://en.wikipedia.org/wiki/Base64
[14]https://developer.mozilla.org/en-US/docs/Web/HTTP/Cookies

What Is R

REST stands for
you can read in
HTTP verbs as c

e.g.

- GET, to rea
- POST, to cr
- PUT, to am
- DELETE, t

The documentatic
interpreted REST

What Tools

Since API stands
with the API to be
well documented a

Also that the input and output from the API are designed for creation and consumption by code - hence the use of formats like JSON and XML.

We can issue API requests from a command line with tools like cURL, which you will see later in this book.

Also GUI tools like Postman, which we cover in a later chapter, allow humans to easily interact with APIs.

When writing application code to interface with an API we are generally able to use a library for the specific programming language that we are working with.

In this book we are using Java and will use the REST Assured library.

Example APIs

16

If you want a very simple API to experiment w
Wars API Web Application.

- swapi.co[16]

This is a very simple API th
Wars characters and plan

The API is well docu
API.

Recor

[15]http://www.ics.uci.edu/~fielding/pubs/dissertation/rest_arch_style.htm

...th at the moment, then I recommend the Star

...t mainly uses GET requests and returns information about Star
...ets.

...mented and has an online GUI that you can use to experiment with the

...mmended Reading

The REST API Tutorial[17] provides a good overview of REST APIs, HTTP Status codes and
Verbs.

Summary

This chapter provided a very high level description of an API (Application Programming
Interface) to differentiate it from a GUI (Graphical User Interface). An API is designed to be
used for systems and applications to communicate, whereas a GUI is designed for humans
to use.

Humans can use API interfaces. Tools such as cURL and Postman can help. We also have the
advantage that for HTTP APIs, the messages are in text format and usually contain human
readable JSON or XML format payloads.

The status codes that are returned when requests are sent to an API help you understand if
the request has been successful (200, 2xx), or if there was something wrong with the request
(4xx), or if something went wrong in the server application (5xx).

At the very least, you should now be familiar with the terms we will be using in this case
study, and have seen some examples of HTTP messages for both requests and responses.

---

[16]https://swapi.co
[17]http://www.restapitutorial.com/

Introducing Tracks Case Study

This Case Study uses a Web Application called Tracks.

Tracks is a Todo Management and Productivity tool with a Web GUI and a REST API. The API uses XML as its Payload format.

This chapter will provide details of why we are using Tracks, where to find the source code and supporting information to help you get started.

Support Page

This book has an on-line support web page:

- compendiumdev.co.uk/page/tracksrestsupport[18]

The web page contains:

- Links to the important websites and tools mentioned.
- Links to the code.
- Links to the Postman collection file.
- Any errata or update information on the book.
- Links to any supporting blog posts.
- Links to any supporting videos.

Some of the web page sections will be mentioned in this book, but others will be added over time as it might be easier to add new content to the web page, than to add it into the book.

---

[18]http://compendiumdev.co.uk/page/tracksrestsupport

How to Use This Case Study

By the time you work through this case study, the version of Tracks will probably have increased. That might mean that some of the information here is out of date. You might not be able to exactly repeat all the steps and see the same results.

If you want to repeat the steps and achieve the same results then you could install the version of Tracks I mention in this book, and possibly the associated software that I used to test it at the time. Tracks is Open Source and the old versions are available to install; but I don't recommend you do that.

Instead, I recommend that you read the text, watch the videos (on the supporting web page), and perform 'looser' experiments. i.e. do the same, or similar things, but don't expect the result to be exactly the same, or look exactly the same, when you do it.

Over the course of the case study I used two versions of tracks: 2.2 and 2.3.

Tracks did change between these versions.

This required changes to the code that I wrote to automate Tracks, and later I'll show you what I changed in the code, and how I investigated the changes.

By the time you come to follow this case study, Tracks may have advanced again, and the code may need to change again.

You may need to change it. Since this is a case study, that is one of the exercises left to you.

Rather than starting from scratch, you can see what and why I created code, then you can change it to work for the current version. You can then take the code forward if you want.

A case study is a time bound body of work. It is what I did at a specific point in time. I'm communicating it so that you can learn from it, and build on it, not so you can repeat it exactly.

Source Code Location

All of the source code for REST Assured and Java mentioned in the book is available on GitHub:

- github.com/eviltester/tracksrestcasestudy[19]

---

[19] https://github.com/eviltester/tracksrestcasestudy

A chapter later in the book called "How to Use the Source Code" describes how to download the source code and install the JAVA SDK and IDE you'll need to run the code.

Case Study Contents Overview

- An overview of the Tracks application and its API
- How to use cURL to explore an API
- How to use Postman to explore an API
- How to use a Proxy to help automate and explore
- How to use REST Assured from Java:
    - Get URLs
    - Post forms
    - REST API testing
        * GET
        * POST
    - XML Response processing
    - JSON Response processing
    - Serialize payload objects to JSON and XML
    - Deserialize JSON and XML to Java objects
- Different stages of code
    - Code that gets something done
    - Code that we re-use
    - Code that we can use for the long term
    - How we refactor between these stages
- Scraping data from other sites to use as test data
- Thought processes and critical evaluation of the work
- Thoughts on REST Assured
- How to improve the code used in this case study
- Exercises for you to try

Why Test Tracks?

Why pick Tracks as an application to test?

Tracks[20] is an open source application written in Ruby on Rails so is relatively easy to install and use. Although, I should mention that, I have always used a pre-built virtual machine from Bitnami or Turnkey (more details later).

Practice Your Testing

I've been aware of Tracks as an application for quite a long time, and I've even experimented with it as a 'real' application i.e. one that I would use to track my TODO lists and manage my work.

I don't use Tracks to manage my work but I do use it as a target for practising my testing.

I've used it:

- personally to practice my testing
- personally to practice automating with WebDriver
- personally to learn new tools and experiment with proxies
- on training courses to provide a 'real' application to automate with WebDriver
- on training courses to provide a target for exploratory testing
- as part of the Black Ops Testing[21] workshops

I've primarily used it to practice testing. I hope that's one reason why you are working through this case study - because you want to practice your testing and improve.

Real Application

Tracks is a 'real' application.

I have built applications which are only used for the purposes of supporting training exercises. These tend to have limitations:

- specific aims - to exhibit particular flaws,
- they tend not to be rich in functionality,
- the GUI probably isn't polished,
- they might be deliberately limited e.g. no database, no security, etc.

---

[20]http://www.getontracks.org/
[21]http://blackopstesting.com

Since Tracks is built for production use it does not have artificial limits, and it changes over time which means that I can keep revisiting it to practice against new functionality.

It also has the type of bugs that slip through the net, some are easy to spot, some are not important, others are harder to spot and you have to work to find them.

Tracks has grown organically over time and isn't as basic as an application designed to be used for teaching testing and automating.

Tracks is built by a dedicated and passionate team of developers in their spare time. They also write a lot of code to help them test so we could review their automated execution coverage and use that to guide our testing.

Rich Functionality

Tracks has a lot of functionality and ways of accessing the functionality that a simpler 'test' application would not have:

- Tracks has a complex GUI.
- Tracks has a REST API.
- Tracks has a mobile GUI interface.
- Tracks is a client/server application.
- Tracks has a database.
- Tracks is multi-user.

Tracks has a complex GUI. The GUI also uses a lot of JavaScript, Ajax calls and DOM updating, this makes it appear more 'modern', but also offers challenges to the tester when automating through the GUI. This also opens up new technologies for the tester to learn.

Tracks has a REST API. Which allows us to experiment with more technical approaches to testing and going behind the GUI to learn new tools and approaches, exploring different risks than the GUI alone offers.

Tracks has a mobile GUI interface. Allowing us to experiment with device based testing in combination with browsers and APIs.

Tracks is a client/server application. Allowing us to focus on the client, or the server side functionality, and the interaction between the two. This also opens up server side logging and server side access. When you are testing a Browser application on a Windows machine and have to connect to a server running in a VM using Linux, you learn to switch between different operating system contexts and have to learn new technology to be able to test.

Tracks has a database. Allowing us to learn how to access it from a GUI tool, or from the command line. We don't have to access the database, but if we extend our testing to encompass the database then we will:

- learn new skills,
- spot new risks to test for,
- have the ability to investigate the cause of defects more deeply,
- manage our environment at a lower level.

Tracks is multi-user. This opens up risks around security, performance, testing under load etc.

Tracks also has the advantage that it is a very focused application, so while it offers a lot of features for testing, it is a small enough domain that we can understand the scope of the application.

Rich Testing Scope

I've been using Tracks as a test target for years. Every time I come to test it I can easily lose myself in it for days at a time.

This case study concentrates on the API and the client server interaction, but in no way does this approach to testing cover everything that Tracks offers. And I have not spent enough time to say that I have learned or tested everything about Tracks.

But I have spent enough time testing Tracks to be able to recommend it as a great testing target, and the time I've spent practising with it, has improved my testing skills and technical skills.

I think the time you spend working through this case study and applying the approaches to Tracks will improve your testing skills. Make sure you apply the techniques and approaches you see here, not just read about it, or watch the videos.

Only application of the approaches will help you advance.

What Is Tracks and GTD?

Tracks is an open source application written in Ruby on Rails which implements the David Allen "Getting Things Done" time management methodology.

- Tracks Home Page - getontracks.org[22]
- Getting Things Done[23]

Getting Things Done

For the purposes of this case study we don't really need to know the Getting Things Done methodology, we do have to understand the entities involved and their relationships, and how Tracks implements them, but if you'd like some additional domain knowledge then I'll cover it here.

GTD is a time management approach with a number of concepts:

- Projects - groups of Tasks which need to be done to implement the project
- Contexts - 'places' where Tasks can be done e.g. @Home, @Shops etc.
- Tasks - have a due date so they can appear on a calendar and you can track slippage or poor schedule estimating. I tend to think of these as TODOs and so I use the term 'Task' and 'TODO' interchangeably.

If you want to learn more about the GTD domain then the following links may also be helpful:

- Lifehacker summary[24]
- Additional documentation on Tracks Wiki[25]

Summary

This is a book about Testing an API as much as it is about Automating an API.

Because APIs seem to be for 'Programmers' we often default to automating the API execution.

But knowing how to interact with the API from the command line with cURL, and with GUI tools such as Postman and HTTP Debug Proxies will increase your ability to test APIs.

In addition, when you do automate the API to support your testing, making sure that the automated code is flexible enough to support Continuous Integration as well as ongoing exploratory testing will help you.

---

[22] http://www.getontracks.org/
[23] https://en.wikipedia.org/wiki/Getting_Things_Done
[24] http://lifehacker.com/productivity-101-a-primer-to-the-getting-things-done-1551880955
[25] https://github.com/TracksApp/tracks/wiki/Help-%26-Support

This case study, although small, covers the thought processes and a variety of practical approaches for supporting your interactive Exploratory Testing, as well as your automated execution.

Installing Tracks

Since we are using Tracks as a learning target we want to find easy ways to install it. I tend to use a pre-built virtual machine.

Because this chapter has the risk of becoming out of date I recommend that you visit the book support page if you experience any install difficulties:

- compendiumdev.co.uk/page/tracksrestsupport[26]

In this chapter I describe:

- how to use the official install from getontracks.org[27],
- pre-built virtual machines from Turnkey[28]
    - my preferred method for runnning Tracks

Official Tracks Install

The Tracks Download page has links to the install instructions. I include this for your reference, but this is not how I install Tracks, I use a Virtual Machine.

- getontracks.org/downloads[29]

The master install documentation is on GitHub:

- github.com/TracksApp/tracks/blob/master/doc/installation.md[30]

Each version may have a slightly different installation process:

---

[26] http://www.compendiumdev.co.uk/page/tracksrestsupport
[27] http://www.getontracks.org
[28] https://www.turnkeylinux.org/tracks
[29] http://www.getontracks.org/downloads/
[30] https://github.com/TracksApp/tracks/blob/master/doc/installation.md

- version 2.2 installation[31]
- version 2.3 installation[32]

You'll need to have Ruby installed, Bundler and a database (MySql, SQLite, PostgreSQL)

- Ruby[33]
- Bundler[34]

It is possible to use the 'official install' instructions with a pre-build 'Ruby' VM from Bitnami[35] or Turnkey. Instructions for installing Tracks into a Bitnami VM are on the book support web page.

Pre-Built Virtual Machines

My main focus with Tracks is having an application to practice testing on.

I prefer to download a pre-built virtual machine with Tracks already installed and running.

Throughout the case studies you will see references to `bitnami` because I used a Virtual Machine from Bitnami, unfortunately Bitnami have discontinued their Tracks VM, leaving Turnkey as the only pre-built Tracks VM that I know of.

Download a pre-build VM from Turnkey:

- Turnkey Tracks[36]

Many of the applications, on which I practice my testing, are run from pre-built virtual machines.

The disadvantage for this case study is that the virtual machines listed on Turnkey will only have one of the versions. Turnkey does not tend to maintain the older versions and make them available for download.

The advantage is that you have to do very little to get them working.

You can also easily install the virtual machines to Cloud instances if you want to have them running separately from your development machine.

---

[31] https://github.com/TracksApp/tracks/blob/2.2_branch/doc/installation.textile
[32] https://github.com/TracksApp/tracks/blob/2.3_branch/doc/installation.md
[33] https://www.ruby-lang.org/en/
[34] http://bundler.io/
[35] https://bitnami.com
[36] https://www.turnkeylinux.org/tracks

Using Virtual Machines

There are a few virtual machine applications that you can use.

- VirtualBox is open source and cross platform
- VMWare is free for some player options but is a commercial product
- Parallels on the Mac is also commercial, I haven't tried it with the virtual machines from Bitnami

I tend to use VMWare. On a Mac I use VMWare Fusion, and on Windows VMWare Workstation.

- vmware.com[37]

This is a paid project, but I find it more reliable.

The virtual machines that you can download from Bitnami and Turnkey will also work on VirtualBox.

- virtualbox.org[38]

VirtualBox is a free virtual machine host.

Turnkey provide a `.vmdk` file which is a Virtual Disk image which you can use with both VMWare and VirtualBox.

Turnkey also provide a `.ova` file which you can open with VirtualBox.

Summary

If we were to actually test the application then we would want to use the official install routines and have a well configured test environment. Since we are using it to practice, we can save ourselves some time and use one of the pre-built options.

I prefer to use virtual machines.

---

[37] http://www.vmware.com

[38] https://www.virtualbox.org

A Tour of Tracks

I have created a video to provide a quick walk-through of the Tracks GUI. You can find it on the book support page video section:

- compendiumdev.co.uk/page/tracksrestsupport[39]

Why Learn the GUI If We Are Testing the API?

Prior to automating an application, or working with its API, I usually try to use it from the GUI first.

I find this makes it easier for me to understand the basic functionality and build a mental model of the application.

I make an exception to this, when the application doesn't have a GUI at all.

Since this is a mental model of the basic application, I simply use it in a browser with no additional tools. I will use an HTTP proxy in a later section. Initially I do not use it with a proxy because I don't want to become too distracted by the HTTP traffic. I use a proxy later when I want to understand the application at a more technical level in preparation for automating it or more technically focused exploratory testing.

Generally I'm doing this to build a model of how the application works and a list of questions and options that I will need to investigate prior to automating.

I'm just doing a quick tour to identify functionality that I can use via the GUI, and then I'll see if I can automate the same functionality using the API. Since we are concentrating on automating using the API, my notes will ignore the Ajax calls and GUI updating.

---

[39]http://compendiumdev.co.uk/page/tracksrestsupport#vtracksoverview

Login

Tracks Login Screen

Login screen to the application, even though every user has their own set of Projects and TODO items.

This suggests I'll need to handle some sort of authentication when using the API. Also, if I were to automate via the API and the GUI at the same time I may be able to share the same session.

This case study used the (now discontinued) Bitnami pre-built virtual machines, the default admin user is 'user' with the password 'bitnami'.

Home Screen

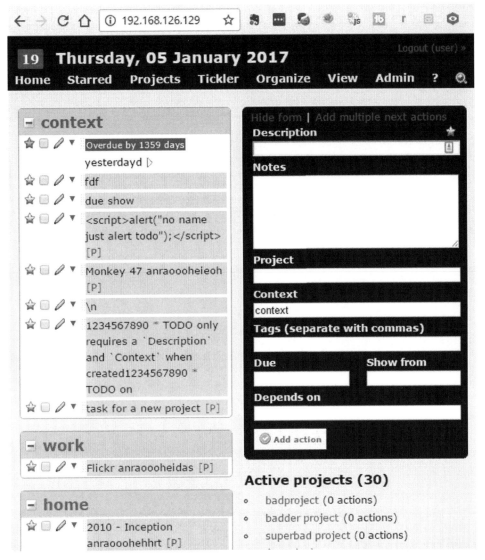

Tracks Home Screen

You can see from the Home screen image that a tester has been using the application, just look at that data!

From the Home screen I can create TODO items (`action`):

- Projects and Contexts are created automatically when added to an `action`.
- Tagging provides another way of categorising and organising TODO items.
- TODO items can be dependent on one another.
- Validation rules applied to `action`,
    - `action` only requires a `Description` and `Context` when created,
    - `action` description length is limited to 100 in the GUI,
        * this is the only HTML validation, any other validation must be applied by the server.

The drop down menu suggests that I can 'star' actions. Since there is a `Starred` menu option.

I can do this on the GUI by clicking the 'star' at the side of the action.

We can edit an `action` in-situ - I assume this is handled via Ajax, which would interesting to automate from the GUI, but we can ignore this since we are concentrating on the API.

Starred Screen

Starred screen shows starred `actions`.

I assume that the API will provide a way of retrieving a list of starred `actions`.

Projects

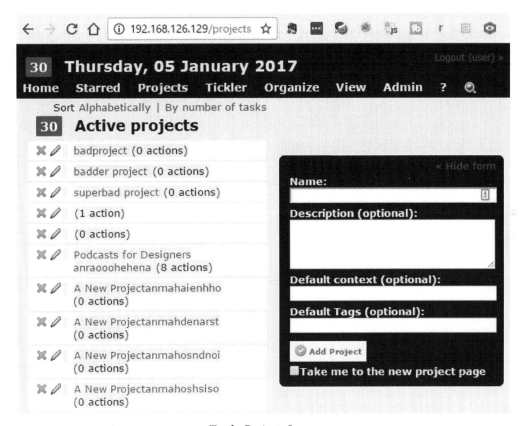

Tracks Projects Screen

Projects shows a list of `project` entities.

Can create a Project from this screen.

Clicking on a Project shows a `project` screen.

Project Edit

Tracks Project Edit Dialog

We can amend the details for a project.

A project can be active, hidden, completed.

A project can be amended after creation to have a description, a default context and tags.

Validation looks as though it is done server-side.

Admin

Tracks Admin Menu

Admin allows editing of user details using Manage Users from the Admin menu.

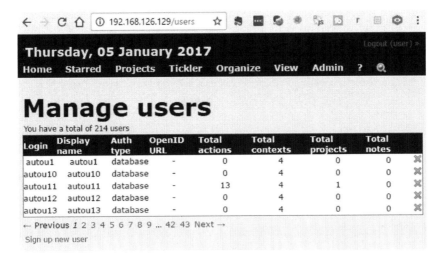

Tracks Manage Users Screen

An Admin user can Manage and create users.

The 'admin' user and the 'normal' user have different options exposed here, so the API should also honour permissions.

Basic Functions to Use and Check in the API

When I test the application I will want to be able to create data in the system to support my testing. So I would like to be able to:

- Create users
- Create `action` and `project` and `context` for users

Basic functionality in the API that I would want to start writing API code to support testing would include:

- Login and authenticate
- Action
    - Create `Action`, and have `context` created automatically
        * Create `action` uses same data validation as GUI
            · `description` is 100 length maximum
            · must have a Context

- List Actions in a Context
- 'Star' an 'Action'
- Retrieve list of 'starred' Actions
- Edit an action
- Project
  - Create Project
    * Add action to existing Project
  - Amend Project
  - Move Project into different status
  - Show actions for a Project
- Admin
  - Create Users
  - User can amend their details (but not another user)

Summary

When an application has a REST API and a GUI, I will use the application via the GUI first to identify the basic functional scope that might be available and to help me understand what entities the application manages and what features it offers.

The Tracks REST API

You can find a video overview of the REST API with cURL on the book support page.

- compendiumdev.co.uk/page/tracksrestsupport[40]

This chapter will provide a short introduction to the terminology and the tools we will initially use, with links to the documentation and downloads. We cover cURL and the REST API in much more detail in a later chapter.

What Is a REST API?

'REST' stands for 'Representational State Transfer.

It basically means an API which uses HTTP and uses the 'HTTP Verbs' (GET, PUT, POST, DELETE, etc.) to retrieve data or amend data through the API. Any data retrieved by a GET would be in the body of the HTTP response, and any data in a PUT or POST request to create and amend data would be in the body of the HTTP request.

You can find information about REST:

- REST Wikipedia page[41]
- An overview REST tutorial at restapitutorial.com[42]
- Roy Fielding[43] defined REST in his Ph.D. Thesis[44], you can read it as a .pdf[45]

---

[40] http://compendiumdev.co.uk/page/tracksrestsupport#vcurloverview

[41] https://en.wikipedia.org/wiki/Representational_state_transfer

[42] http://www.restapitutorial.com/

[43] https://www.ics.uci.edu/~fielding/

[44] http://www.ics.uci.edu/~fielding/pubs/dissertation/top.htm

[45] https://www.ics.uci.edu/~fielding/pubs/dissertation/fielding_dissertation.pdf

Tracks REST API Documentation

The Tracks API documentation is in the application itself.

From the ? menu, the REST API Docs menu.

The 'REST API Docs' menu

Clicking this takes us to a page with the API documentation.

For easier future reference I make a note of the URL.

URL docs located at /integrations/rest_api

- /integrations/rest_api

API Doc Examples

The API documentation is fairly minimal but it does have some examples - in cURL

- cURL official page[46]
- cURL Wikipedia description[47]

One of the things I will want to do is try the examples using cURL, before I try and use the API in other tools. This way I can learn if the API examples work as documented before

---

[46] https://curl.haxx.se/
[47] https://en.wikipedia.org/wiki/CURL

trying to translate them to another tool. If I can use the API via cURL then I can translate the examples to any other mechanism later.

From the documentation I can see that:

- System uses Basic HTTP Authentication for the API
    - This is different from the main application, which uses a logged on session cookie
- Message content is XML
- `GET` is used to retrieve data
- `DELETE` is used to delete data
- `PUT` is used to amend data
- `POST` is used to create data
    - If we are not familiar with cURL then it is hard to tell from the cURL request that `POST` is used

The following endpoints are used:

- `/todos.xml`
- `/todos/ID.xml`
- `/tickler.xml`
- `/done.xml`
- `/hidden.xml`
- `/calendar.xml`
- `/contexts.xml`
- `/contexts/ID.xml`
- `/contexts/ID/todos.xml`
- `/projects.xml`
- `/projects/ID.xml`
- `/projects/ID/todos.xml`

The documentation says that we can also limit returned information to the 'index' fields: `ID`, `created_at`, `modified_at`, `completed_at`. We do this by adding `?limit_fields=index` to the request.

We can get only active TODOs by adding a parameter `?limit_to_active_todos=1`.

Omissions in API Documentation

`user.xml` or `users.xml` is not mentioned as an endpoint so we might not be able to create or amend users through the API.

Also I suspect we might be able to have more 'limit' type parameter combinations.

General HTTP REST Return Codes

When we issue REST calls, there are a few HTTP return codes we would expect to see:

- 200 (OK) when we `GET` to retrieve information
- 401 (Unauthorized) when we try to access information without the correct credentials e.g. without logging in
- 404 (Not Found) when we `GET` information that does not exist, or `POST`, `PUT` `DELETE` to an end point that does not exist
- 201 (created) when we use `POST` to create a new entity
- 409 (Already Exists) we we try to create an existing entity
- 302 (Redirect) when we successfully issue a request, the system may redirect us somewhere else, e.g `POST` a login request and be redirected to the user dashboard

Useful information on HTTP Status Codes can be found at:

- httpstatuses.com[48]

Summary

The Tracks REST API is well documented, with examples of how to trigger it interactively.

Testing an application to ensure that it conforms to the documentation is an important part of any testing process, in addition to helping us learn and understand the system.

Although the Tracks REST API only uses XML, I do cover JSON processing in a later chapter.

---

[48]https://httpstatuses.com/

Using a Proxy to View GUI Traffic

Before I start using cURL and working with the API, I want to first check if the GUI itself uses the API.

I check by using the GUI in a browser, while all the browser traffic is captured by an HTTP Proxy.

You can find a video overview of using Tracks through a proxy in the book support page videos:

- compendiumdev.co.uk/page/tracksrestsupport[49]

Why?

I do this because, having read the documentation on the API, I now know what an API call looks like.

If the GUI itself uses the API then when we test or automate through the API we have also covered a lot of the GUI to server interaction. This would allow us to reduce the automated coverage that we might want to achieve through GUI automated execution.

If the GUI does not use API calls, then it suggests that the application may have multiple implementations of the same functionality. Or, possibly more than one route to the same functionality. Either way, we probably have to continue to test the same functionality through the GUI, as we do through the API.

In order to make a technically informed decision about the risk we would have to review the code, rather than rely on information obtained from observing the HTTP traffic.

How?

The easiest HTTP Proxies to use are:

---

[49] http://compendiumdev.co.uk/page.php?title=tracksrestsupport#vproxy

- For Windows: Fiddler[50]
- For Mac: Charles[51]

Both of these are 'easiest' because they hook in to the Operating System HTTP connections and start listening to traffic by default without any configuration.

You could also use:

- OWASP ZAP Proxy[52]
- BurpSuite Free Edition[53]

Both of these are free, and cross platform projects (they require a Java Runtime Edition installed). You have to do a little extra configuration in the browser to amend the network connection settings to use a proxy.

- Firefox Network Connection Configuration[54]
- Chrome Proxy Configuration[55]
- IE Proxy Configuration[56]

This 'how to' article[57] details proxy configuration for different browsers.

Viewing Traffic

Assuming that you have installed the proxy correctly:

- You have a browser installed.
- You have one of the proxy tools installed.
- The proxy tool is running.
- The browser is running.

---

[50] http://www.telerik.com/fiddler

[51] https://www.charlesproxy.com/

[52] https://www.owasp.org/index.php/OWASP_Zed_Attack_Proxy_Project

[53] https://portswigger.net/burp/download.html

[54] https://support.mozilla.org/en-US/kb/advanced-panel-settings-in-firefox#w_connection

[55] https://support.google.com/chrome/answer/96815?hl=en-GB

[56] http://windows.microsoft.com/en-gb/windows/change-internet-explorer-proxy-server-settings

[57] http://www.howto-connect.com/windows-10-customize-proxy-server-settings-in-browsers/

- The browser is configured to use the proxy.
- When you visit the URL for your tracks installation, the site still loads.

We can then start viewing and analysing the traffic to see if API URLs are used.

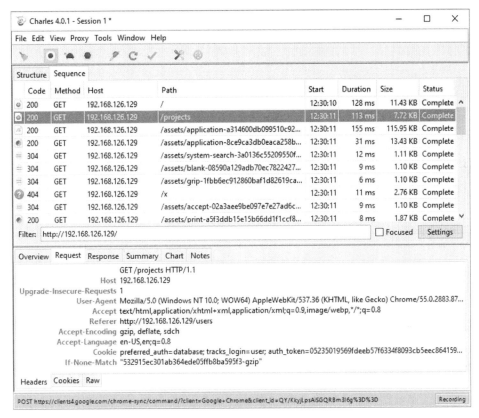

Viewing Traffic in Charles Proxy

When I use the application and:

- Login.
- Create an `action`.
- Create a `project`.
- Visit different parts of the GUI to see lists of entities.
- Amend an `action`.
- Amend a `project`.

- Delete an `action`.
- Delete a `project`.

I can see that only `POST` and `GET` are used, and none of the URLs are `.xml` URLs, so different parts of the application are being called, the API is not used by the GUI.

Implications

For our purposes of learning how to use the API, it means that we don't have any examples in the Proxy of the calls and results used for the API.

Which means that we have to rely on the documentation showing us how to use the API, rather than having 'live' examples taken from the actual application itself.

Summary

Use the GUI, with traffic directed through a proxy, to see if the GUI is using the API.

If the GUI is using the API then we have examples of the API calls being used. This might help us better understand the API or possibly spot any undocumented functionality. We might even spot nuanced usage that wasn't clear from the documentation.

If the GUI is not using the API then we are aware that testing the API in isolation does not mitigate all the risk associated with server side application functionality. The server side functionality is triggered in at least two ways: the GUI made HTTP calls and the REST API calls. This increases the potential scope of testing.

Using a Proxy and Fuzzer to Create Users

An Admin user can use the 'Manage Users' functionality to create users.

When we test and automate an application it can help to have a lot of users to work with.

At the moment we haven't investigated how to automate the application with code, but we have seen how to interact with the application using a Proxy.

An HTTP Proxy allows us to:

- Capture requests.
- Resend requests.
- Edit requests prior to resending them.

And some HTTP Proxies allow us to:

- Fuzz a request,
    - resend a request multiple times and vary the data for each sent request.

This is normally used for security testing to brute force requests with vulnerable payloads. e.g. SQL injection payloads, or XSS payloads.

If we can edit the request that creates a user and resend it, then we might be able to use a Fuzzer to resend the request multiple times and create multiple users.

You can find a video overview of the creation of Users with a Proxy Fuzzer on the book support page.

- compendiumdev.co.uk/page/tracksrestsupport[58]

---

[58]http://compendiumdev.co.uk/page/tracksrestsupport#vfuzzdata

Tools

I will use:

- Charles Proxy[59] for the initial investigation of the request resending
  - although any HTTP Proxy could be used for this.
- Foxy Proxy Standard Chrome Plugin[60] to make it easier to configure Chrome Browser to use a proxy
  - although I could use the proxy settings in Chrome to do this.
- OpenOffice Calc Spreadsheet[61] to create data
  - although I could use any spreadsheet to do this e.g. LibreOffice[62], MS Excel, Google Sheets[63].
- OWASP ZAP Proxy[64] as a Proxy with Fuzzer
  - although I could have used BurpSuite[65] to do this.

Capture and Resend the Create User Request

I can use Charles to capture the HTTP request made when creating a User through the GUI:

- Have Chrome running.
- Run Charles Proxy.
- Make sure requests are being captured in Charles Proxy.
- Have Tracks running.
- Login to Tracks as Admin user.
- Use 'Admin > Manage Users' then 'Sign up new user' to create a User.
- Capture the request in Charles.

---

[59] https://www.charlesproxy.com
[60] https://chrome.google.com/webstore/detail/foxyproxy-standard/gcknhkkoolaabfmlnjonogaaifnjlfnp?hl=en
[61] https://www.openoffice.org/product/calc.html
[62] http://www.libreoffice.org/
[63] https://www.google.co.uk/sheets/about/
[64] https://www.owasp.org/index.php/OWASP_Zed_Attack_Proxy_Project
[65] https://portswigger.net/burp/

Create a New User using Tracks GUI

302	POST	192.168.126.129	/users	11:04:33	256 ms	2.72 KB	Complete
⊙ 200	GET	192.168.126.129	/users\page=35	11:04:33	75 ms	5.65 KB	Complete
≡ 304	GET	192.168.126.129	/assets/application-8ce9ca3db0eaca258b...	11:04:33	6 ms	1.41 KB	Complete
≡ 304	GET	192.168.126.129	/assets/application-a314600db099510c92...	11:04:33	6 ms	1.40 KB	Complete
≡ 304	GET	192.168.126.129	/assets/system-search-3a0136c55209550f...	11:04:33	3 ms	1.42 KB	Complete
≡ 304	GET	192.168.126.129	/assets/blank-08590a129adb70ec7822427...	11:04:33	3 ms	1.41 KB	Complete

Filter: 192.168.126.129   ☐ Focused   Settings

Overview   Request   Response   Summary   Chart   Notes

POST /users HTTP/1.1
Host: 192.168.126.129
Content-Length: 174
Cache-Control: max-age=0
Origin: http://192.168.126.129
Upgrade-Insecure-Requests: 1
User-Agent: Mozilla/5.0 (Windows NT 10.0; WOW64) AppleWebKit/537.36 (KHTML, like Gecko) Chrome/55.0.2883.87 Safari/537.36
Content-Type: application/x-www-form-urlencoded
Accept: text/html,application/xhtml+xml,application/xml;q=0.9,image/webp,*/*;q=0.8
Referer: http://192.168.126.129/signup
Accept-Encoding: gzip, deflate
Accept-Language: en-US,en;q=0.8

Cookie: tracks_login=user; auth_token=05235019569fdeeb57f6334f8093cb5eec864159; _tracksapp_session=TVpvMHpYbS9LWEpwRWlo
UnhmeTRKK0tsVmNCa1FQaGRCZDINa3Z2SXdkZXpTdlFSc0RmRHdZbXIaaHFUTTZuZzkyTitwR0tqNVlaOU9rdFAxcHNSVE9GbTN5WII2dC
9YZ0xOeDRFL0RRQ2VrTmswT1ludmtsc3FKNHdnUGNsd1dzNGlGblVoTFUva3FZNjV5L1pVbzlRRVJWJWTjdPNDVhUy8zdFZROWJuRUNQbzk5
QWFQNDNIT0VHTFkrR1pxWU1KeXlyRmRqR05oQXNtdFFqYkJFMnU1Z2RyNExUL2JLdkJHTU5xeEkzMldNbzhPbmY5ZHo1YmRUWEcvRVp
3RjgwdWp4UGk5b2Z2dWURYR1NXOThwR0dyUE8vYTdrMEtIYIU4bEpGcnICY0FCSDBuSFF0WE5DTER4R2svOG1KN2
QxS0ovVUJncWt1azZINWJ6dmRjcWJzV2xFNnlNc0E0UXFqa3JUZWIKZ3hhUx2Y2tKRINyQVBBQitqT29TK1IpU3FOc0Q5WDA5UDJjV3RlQV
kvYzBLeC9BeWhVZDgrTk40az0tLXJkSHJ5YIBjR1VMSjRpZ1hzT01jmc9PQ%3D%3D--cee0d57332ee0f819342f2a559dd6f24e6784369

utf8=%E2%9C%93&authenticity_token=IAUhgqc6ElokzWNFCerK15CEnUTpFzrrGyi5N0IGvko%3D&user%5Blogin%5D=alan5555&user%
5Bpassword%5D=alan5555&user%5Bpassword_confirmation%5D=alan5555

Capture Create User HTTP Request in Charles Proxy

- Once I have the HTTP request in Charles I can right click on the request to 'Compose'

a new request
- Select Form view to make editing the request easier.
- Amend the HTTP request to edit the username.
- Click 'Execute' button to send the new request.

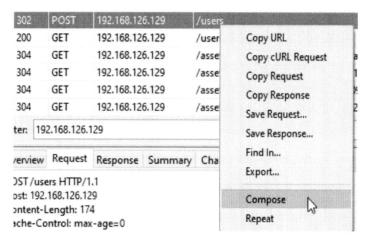

Compose a new Request in Charles

Select Form View

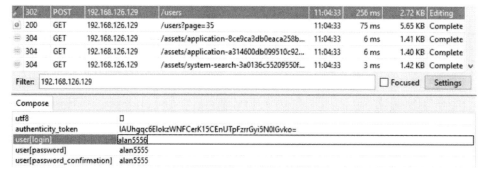

Edit the Details in the Form to have a new username

Execute The Request To Send it

- I double check that the user is created by opening a new Chrome Incognito Window.
- Visit Tracks GUI in the Incognito Window.
- Login to Tracks as the newly created user.
- I also refresh the 'Manage Users' List in the non-incognito Chrome session to check that the number of users has increased.

We Learned

By doing this, we learned that it is possible to resend a 'create user' request with different user details to create another user.

This means that the authentication token and cookies are re-usable within the request.

It also means that I can do the same thing in a Fuzzer to automatically replace the username with different values and create a series of users.

I will use OWASP ZAP Proxy as the Fuzzer to create users.

Using OWASP ZAP Proxy

The OWASP ZAP Proxy is written in Java so is compatible cross platform with Windows, Linux and Mac.

You can download OWASP ZAP and follow the install instructions[66] from the official site.

On Windows, although it adds a '.exe' I sometimes experience GUI issues (where I can't click on tabs in the GUI interface) when I run it this way, so I usually go to the installed program folder and run the '.bat' file. But you might not need to do this, try the installed '.exe' launcher first.

OWASP ZAP does not automatically hook in to the operating system and act as a default Proxy so we have to configure the browser to use OWASP ZAP.

---

[66] https://github.com/zaproxy/zaproxy/wiki/Downloads

We can configure the browser by amending the browser's proxy settings. But I tend to use FoxyProxy Standard as a plugin to manage the settings.

When a proxy starts, it 'listens' on a particular HTTP Port for HTTP Requests, which it captures before forwarding on to the default internet connection. We have to configure our browser to use the Proxy Port instead of the default Operating System HTTP port.

We can find out what port the OWASP ZAP Proxy is 'listening on' in the OWASP ZAP 'Local Proxy' Options:

- Use the 'Tools' Menu.
- Select 'Options...'.
- Select the 'Local Proxy' item in Options.
- Make a note of the 'Address' - usually `localhost`.
- Make a note of the 'Port' - often `8080` mine is set to `8888`.
- Use these values in your browser configuration to configure the Proxy.

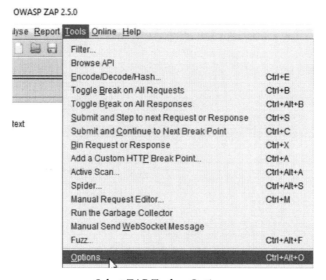

Select ZAP Tools > Options

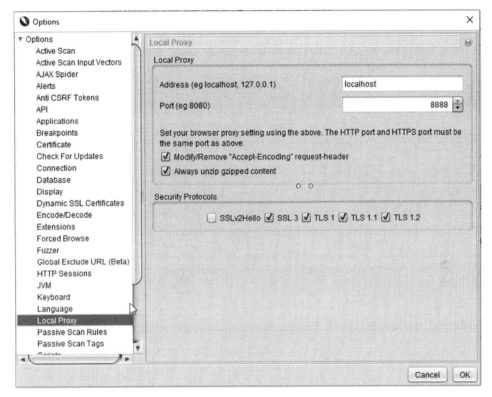

ZAP Options - Local Proxy

Capture Traffic in ZAP and Use the Fuzzer

Use the Tracks GUI once more to make sure that the requests are displayed in ZAP and are being captured.

After you have created a user in Tracks, find the request in ZAP so you know how to identify it, then use the Fuzzer.

- Use the 'Tools' Menu.
- Select 'Fuzz...'.
- View the 'Select Message' dialog.
- Find and select the POST message that was used to Create a User.

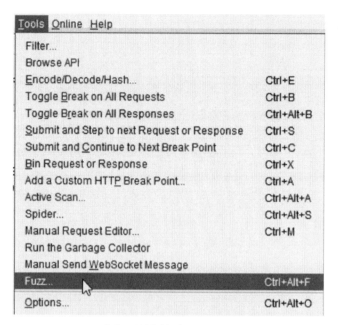

Select ZAP Tools > Fuzz...

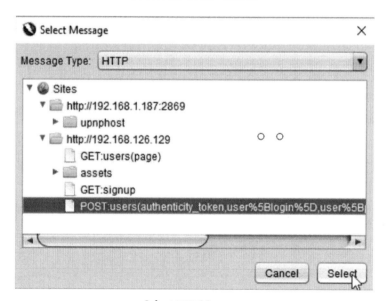

Select POST Message

In the Fuzzer dialog:

- Highlight the part of the message that you wish to replace with 'fuzzed' values.
- Select the 'Add' button on Fuzz Locations.
- Add a Payload.
- Add the list of Strings you want to use as the payload, with each value on a new line e.g.

```
alan8889
alan8890
alan8891
etc.
```

- Before starting the Fuzzer, make sure the 'Delay' Options are set.
  - I amend the 'Delay when fuzzing' to be 1000 milliseconds to add a gap of 1 second between sending each request.
  - Without this the requests are sent one after another, without any delay between them, and you can overload the server.
- Start the Fuzzer.

Highlight part of message and Add Fuzz Location

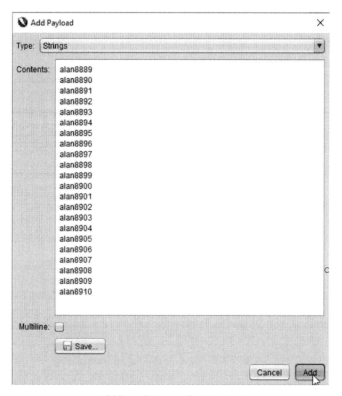

Add list of Strings for Payload

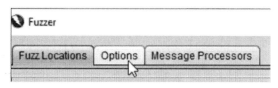

Check Fuzzer Options

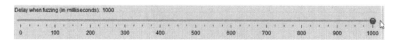

Set 'Delay when fuzzing' Options

Start Fuzzer

You will see the Fuzzer start to send requests, one every second:

- The Fuzzer dialog shows the progress.
- Each fuzz request shows the response status code.
- The data sent in the payload can be seen in the payload column.

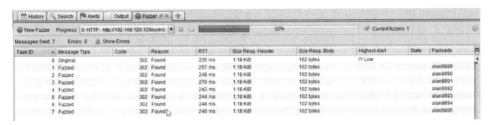

Fuzzer in progress

You can view the actual requests and responses:

- Click on each of the fuzz requests.
- View the 'Request' and 'Response' details in the main GUI.

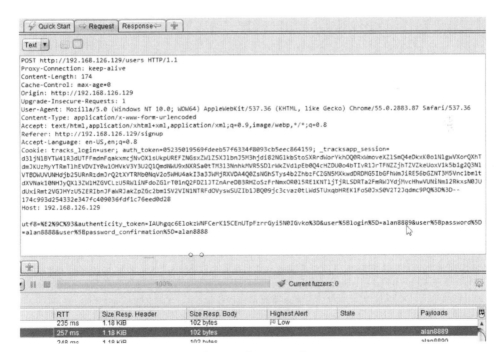

View Fuzzed Requests Sent

Multiple Users Created

Using a Fuzzer can be a very useful way to use a 'hacking' tool as a Test Data Population tool.

Different fuzzers have different capabilities, and it is possible to use the fuzzers to create random data if necessary.

The BurpSuite Fuzzer is also very capable and worth experimenting with.

Quick Tip - Creating Data in a Spreadsheet

In the example above I created a list of usernames:

```
alan8889
alan8890
alan8891
etc.
```

I actually created those in a spreadsheet. Any spreadsheet will do, but I tend to use either Google Sheet, OpenOffice or LibreOffice.

To create data:

- Type a value into one of the cells e.g. alan8889.
- Select the bottom right hand corner of the cell.
- Drag the mouse down to the number of cells you require.
- When you release the mouse the spreadsheet will increment the data you created.
- Copy and paste the values of the cells into the payload edit screen in the Proxy.

View Fuzzed Requests Sent

Summary

I used quite a lot of screenshots in this chapter because if you haven't seen the Proxies in use, and haven't tried Fuzzing before, then it can be hard to follow the instructions.

That's also why I created a video to support this chapter.

- compendiumdev.co.uk/page/tracksrestsupport[67]

Fuzzing is a hacking technique but I often use it like this to quickly create data in the System Under Test, or explore a particular request with a set of data that I'm interested in.

Often I'll conduct Exploratory Testing on a system without having any automated abstractions, or code to help me, and Proxies play a big part in my testing approach.

Using Fuzzers helps me increase the data coverage I can use without extensive tool support and without having to write a lot of code to automate the application.

---

[67]http://compendiumdev.co.uk/page/tracksrestsupport#vfuzzdata

Case Study Example Using cURL on Tracks

The API documentation for Tracks lists examples of how to call the API. The examples all use a command line tool called cURL and they look like the following:

```
$ curl -u username:p4ssw0rd -H "Content-Type: text/xml" \
    http://192.168.17.129/contexts.xml
```

This command looks complicated but I will explain it in this chapter.

What Is cURL?

cURL[68] is a command line tool for making HTTP requests.

cURL is open source, free, cross platform and available on Mac, Windows and Linux.

It is often used in command line scripting for downloading and uploading files and data.

cURL would not normally be the entry point for learning how to use or Automate an API, but since the examples for Tracks all use cURL it seems like a sensible place to start as we should really check if the documented examples for the API actually work.

Since all the Tracks API examples use cURL, we can use the Tracks documentation to help us learn cURL.

Case Study Details

The following sections describe the setup of my environment used for the examples in this chapter.

Tracks

I was running tracks in a VM from Bitnami on ip address 192.168.1.126.

---

[68]https://curl.haxx.se

Tracks REST API Documentation

Tracks API documentation is available within the system.

```
http://192.168.1.126/integrations/rest_api
```

All examples in the Tracks documentation use cURL.

Installing cURL

First check if you have cURL installed by typing `curl --version` into a command line or terminal.

```
D:\Users\Alan\Documents>curl --version

curl 7.39.0 (x86_64-pc-win32) libcurl/7.39.0
OpenSSL/1.0.1g zlib/1.2.8 WinIDN libssh2/1.4.3
Protocols: dict file ftp ftps gopher http https
imap imaps ldap pop3 pop3s rtsp scp sftp smtp
smtps telnet tftp
Features: AsynchDNS IDN IPv6 Largefile SSPI
SPNEGO NTLM SSL libz
```

If you have cURL installed then you'll see something like the above (from my Windows machine), where cURL reports the version and the capabilities of that version.

If you don't have cURL installed then follow the download and installation instructions from curl.haxx.se/download.html[69].

The cURL project provides a 'wizard' to help with the download so you can choose the different options and it will guide you to the most appropriate download.

- curl.haxx.se/dlwiz[70]

I recommend that you choose a download that has SSL and SSH enabled.

On Mac you can use Homebrew to install cURL[71]

---

[69] https://curl.haxx.se/download.html

[70] https://curl.haxx.se/dlwiz

[71] http://brewformulas.org/Curl

```
brew install curl
```

cURL has extensive documentation available. This case study does not attempt to cover all the functionality available within cURL. You can read the documentation on the cURL web site.

curl.haxx.se/docs[72]

Reading the Examples in Tracks Documentation

The following is one of the examples listed on the Tracks documentation page:

```
$ curl -u username:p4ssw0rd -H "Content-Type: text/xml" \
      http://192.168.17.129/contexts.xml

  >> <?xml version="1.0" encoding="UTF-8"?>
  <contexts>...</contexts>
```

This shows the:

- command prompt $
- a line continuation or 'split' character \ to allow the command to be written across multiple lines
- the response from the command >>

So the actual command entered is the following:

```
curl -u username:p4ssw0rd -H "Content-Type: text/xml" \
      http://192.168.17.129/contexts.xml
```

The representation on the web site has a \ as the trailing character, because the entire command is designed to be treated as one command at the command line, but for readability on-line has been split across multiple lines.

The above command should work on Linux or Mac, but will fail on Windows. Windows uses ^ as the 'split' character.

On Windows the command would be typed as follows:

---

[72] https://curl.haxx.se/docs

```
curl -u username:p4ssw0rd -H "Content-Type: text/xml" ^
    http://192.168.17.129/contexts.xml
```

It could be written in one line without the split character. In this book the line would go over the edge of the page (hence the reason the 'split' character is used in the first place). To show it on one line below, I have replaced username with name, p4ssw0rd with pwd and shortened the IP address in the URL and written ip instead of 192.168.17.129 i.e.

```
curl -u name:pwd -H "Content-Type: text/xml" http://ip/contexts.xml
```

I draw this to your attention because I have seen people trying to follow the REST API examples and assume that the documentation or cURL is broken, when in fact they are just not used to cURL and so misread the documentation.

Common issues I've seen are:

- Entering the $ prefixing the command in the documentation.
- Trying to use \ at the Windows command line.
- Trying to use https addresses without the SSL version of cURL.

Remember, if you are on Windows use ^ instead of \ at the end of lines where the command splits across lines in the documentation.

Try the Tracks API Examples

When working with an API the first thing we want to do is try the examples and make sure they work.

For the Tracks examples, this is pretty simple, I can copy and paste them from the web page into my console e.g. the example given for retrieving all the Contexts is listed on the page as:

```
curl -u username:p4ssw0rd -H "Content-Type: text/xml" \
    http://192.168.1.126/contexts.xml
```

Tracks has even added the correct IP address, making it easy to try.

Obviously I need to amend the username and password to be that of the user in my tracks installation.

I've kept it simple and insecure so my username is 'user' and my password is 'bitnami'.

```
curl -u user:bitnami -H "Content-Type: text/xml" \
    http://192.168.1.126/contexts.xml
```

If I was on Windows I would type:

```
curl -u user:bitnami -H "Content-Type: text/xml" ^
    http://192.168.1.126/contexts.xml
```

This returns an XML response, and since my installation has no 'Contexts' the XML has no real detail:

```
<?xml version="1.0" encoding="UTF-8"?>
<nil-classes type="array"/>
```

But I have an XML response, so the example 'worked'.

A Few Extra Points to Note About Windows

The \ works for this purpose on Linux and Mac, but not on Windows.

To have the command work on Windows, I either amend it so the command is on a single line, or replace the \ with ^

```
curl -u user:bitnami -H "Content-Type: text/xml" ^
    http://192.168.1.126/contexts.xml
```

Pasting the above into a Windows command line has the desired result of being treated as a single command:

```
curl -u user:bitnami -H "Content-Type: text/xml" ^
More? http://192.168.1.126/contexts.xml

<?xml version="1.0" encoding="UTF-8"?>
<nil-classes type="array"/>
```

You can see in the above listing that the Windows console prints `More?` after the 'caret' ^ and then accepts the rest of the pasted content from the input.

Understanding the Example

Let's make sure we understand the example:

```
curl -u user:bitnami -H "Content-Type: text/xml" \
    http://192.168.1.126/contexts.xml
```

- No HTTP verb is specified so GET is used by default.
- -u user:bitnami - specified that the request should use HTTP Basic Authentication with a username of user and password of bitnami.
- -H "Content-Type: text/xml" - specified that a Content-Type header should be added of type text/xml.
- http://192.168.1.126/contexts.xml the URL we want cURL to GET.

Exploring the Example

What happens if we don't add the authentication?

```
curl -H "Content-Type: text/xml" http://192.168.1.126/contexts.xml
```

We receive the response:

```
192.168.1.126/contexts.xml
Login unsuccessful.
```

So we know that authentication is required.

What happens if we don't add the Content-Type: header?

```
curl -u user:bitnami http://192.168.1.126/contexts.xml
```

We receive the response:

```
<?xml version="1.0" encoding="UTF-8"?>
<nil-classes type="array"/>
```

Which looks like we don't really need to pass in the Content-Type: header.

Note: If I was testing this application I might choose to ignore the Content-Type: header and not pass it in with any of my requests. But there is a risk that this might not be a valid assumption. Therefore if I found a potential bug when sending a request, I would probably have to resend the request with the Content-Type: header present, just to double check that the absence of the header was not the problem.

Tracks GET **API Calls**

Tracks documentation has a list of API calls which can be used with GET

- /todos.xml
- /todos/ID.xml - where ID is the id of a TODO, to retrieve a single TODO
- /done.xml
- /hidden.xml
- /calendar.xml
- /contexts.xml
- /contexts/ID.xml - where ID is the id of a Context, to retrieve a single Context
- /contexts/ID/todos.xml - where ID is the id of a Context, to retrieve the TODOs for a Context
- /projects.xml
- /projects/ID.xml - where ID is the id of a Project, to retrieve a single Project
- /projects/ID/todos.xml - where ID is the id of a Project, to retrieve the TODOs for a Project

The GET calls are not particularly useful until we can create data, except to demonstrate that the application is in fact, empty of data.

So we will revisit the GET calls after we have created some data.

Adding Data

Adding data in Tracks is done using the POST command.

The examples on the page show the creation of a Project, and a TODO.

To Create a Project

```
curl -u user:bitnami -H "Content-Type: text/xml" \
    -d "<project><name>A Project</name></project>" \
    http://192.168.1.126/projects.xml -i
```

New options in the above request:

- -d - adds the string as the request body and sets the request type to POST.
- -i - shows the response headers.

Why do we want to see the response headers?

Because the status code tells us if the response was successful.

```
Status: 201 Created
```

The status is also summarised as the first line in the output as:

```
>> HTTP/1.1 201 Created
```

And the Location header tells us the id of the Project.

```
Location: http://192.168.1.126/projects/13
```

Without the -i nothing is written to stdout. Therefore we don't know if the Project was created (shown by the status header) or the id number of the Project (shown in the Location header). We would have to use the GUI to tell us, or issue a GET request on http://192.168.1.126/projects.xml and review the list of returned projects.

To Create a TODO on the Project

The example in the documentation lists the following cURL request to create a TODO:

```
curl -u user:bitnami -H "Content-Type: text/xml" \
    -d "<todo><description>Do This</description> \
    <context_id>2</context_id> \
    <project_id>65</project_id></todo>" \
    http://192.168.1.126/todos.xml -i
```

We already know how to find the id of the Project, but how do we know the id of the Context?

Since my Project was created with id 13, I'll use this in the request, and since I don't know the Context, I'll try without the context attribute.

```
curl -u user:bitnami -H "Content-Type: text/xml" \
    -d "<todo><description>Do This</description><project_id>13</project_id></todo>" \
    http://192.168.1.126/todos.xml -i
```

Oops. Based on the response below, the `context` attribute can't be missing or blank.

```
HTTP/1.1 409 Conflict
. . .
Status: 409 Conflict
. . .
Content-Type: text/html; charset=UTF-8

<?xml version="1.0" encoding="UTF-8"?>
<errors>
  <error>Context can't be blank</error>
</errors>
```

OK, so I'll add a `context` with `id` of 2 and see what happens.

```
curl -u user:bitnami -H "Content-Type: text/xml" \
    -d "<todo><description>Do This</description> \
    <context_id>2</context_id> \
    <project_id>13</project_id></todo>" \
    http://192.168.1.126/todos.xml -i
```

Oops. Context is unknown.

```
HTTP/1.1 409 Conflict
. . .
Status: 409 Conflict
. . .
Content-Type: text/html; charset=UTF-8

<?xml version="1.0" encoding="UTF-8"?>
<errors>
  <error>Context unknown</error>
</errors>
```

This is slightly different behaviour than we observed in the GUI. In the GUI we used the names of Contexts and Projects and the Context was automatically created when we added it in the `action` creation. It doesn't look as though we can do that through the API.

What to Do When the API Documentation Is Incomplete?

Documentation is often incomplete. And as testers, we have to learn to work around that.

On a 'real' project we will be able to ask someone, and hopefully they will be able to tell us.

But sometimes we will be trying to automate an application for which we have minimal support. Or possibly a tool that we have inherited. So we have to be able to figure this out.

In this case the answer is pretty simple. We just create a Context, and then we know what the id is.

We have learned some of the relational dependencies in the data model. Project and Context are both top level entities. But a TODO depends on a Project and a Context.

We could have learned this the 'hard' way, by experimenting with the API and trying different combinations of attributes until we hit upon a combination that worked. But we already knew this because we used the GUI for Tracks and we saw this dependency from the GUI.

The 'Create Project' form just has Name with optional Description and optional tags.

The 'Create Action' (modelled in the API as a TODO), requires a description and a project, and a context. As suggested by the error message.

Maintain Referential Integrity

Very often when testing APIs we do want to test whether referential integrity is maintained, and we can do this by trying to create entities in the wrong order.

In this case, we can see that Tracks has code to check for referential integrity, so we need to create a Context first.

Create a Context

The API documentation page does not tell us what the XML for a Context looks like.

The GUI suggests that a Context is created with the name, so I could just try and create one.

```
curl -u user:bitnami -H "Content-Type: text/xml" \
    -d "<context><name>Work</name></context>" \
    http://192.168.1.126/contexts.xml -i
```

That worked, and I can see that the Context was created with id 1:

```
HTTP/1.1 201 Created
...
Location: http://192.168.1.126/contexts/1
...
Status: 201 Created
...
Content-Type: text/html; charset=UTF-8
```

If this had not worked then I would have created a Context using the GUI and issued a GET on the contexts.xml API to see how Tracks modelled the Context in XML. i.e.

```
curl -u user:bitnami -H "Content-Type: text/xml" \
    http://192.168.1.126/contexts.xml
```

And I would have seen:

```
<contexts type="array">
  <context>
    <created-at type="datetime">2015-01-09T14:58:21+00:00</created-at>
    <hide type="boolean">false</hide>
    <id type="integer">1</id>
    <name>Work</name>
    <position type="integer">0</position>
    <updated-at type="datetime">2015-01-09T14:58:21+00:00</updated-at>
  </context>
</contexts>
```

Creating Multiple Items

At this point we already know how to create single items from the command line.

But how do we create multiple items from the command line?

I could create multiple requests, but is there an 'easy' way?

Assuming we don't want to install any other software we need to turn to the shell, with examples below for Mac, Linux and Windows. These examples are designed to be typed into the command line, I would have to write them differently if I wanted to add them into a batch or shell script.

On Mac and Linux

We can use Bash to create a simple loop over the contents of a file called 'projects.txt'.

The `projects.txt` file would be a simple list of names e.g.

```
projectone
projecttwo
projectthree
```

Each line of the file is read from `projects.txt` as a stream and the line itself used in the command as $pname

```
while read pname; \
do \
curl -u user:bitnami -H "Content-Type: text/xml" \
-d "<project><name>$pname</name></project>" \
http://192.168.1.126/projects.xml -i; \
done < projects.txt
```

On Windows

```
FOR /F "delims=" %i in (projects.txt) ^
do ^
curl -u user:bitnami -H "Content-Type: text/xml" ^
-d "<project><name>%i</name></project>" ^
http://192.168.1.126/projects.xml -i
```

Amending Data

Amending data in Tracks requires a message sent with a PUT HTTP Verb.

Since we can retrieve data using the GET commands, the easiest way to amend the data is to first of all retrieve the XML for the entity we want to amend. Then change the XML, and PUT it back.

The API essentially supports the following:

- `/todos.xml`
- `/todos/ID.xml` - where `ID` is the `id` of a TODO, to retrieve a single TODO
- `/tickler.xml`
- `/todos/done.xml` - *docs say /done.xml*
- `/hidden.xml` - Have not been able to get this working yet
- `/calendar.xml`
- `/contexts.xml`
- `/contexts/ID.xml` - where `ID` is the `id` of a Context, to retrieve a single Context
- `/contexts/ID/todos.xml` - where `ID` is the `id` of a Context, to retrieve the TODO for a Context
- `/projects.xml`
- `/projects/ID.xml` - where `ID` is the `id` of a Project, to retrieve a single Project
- `/projects/ID/todos.xml` - where `ID` is the `id` of a Project, to retrieve the TODO for a Project

Amending Projects

Get the data you want:

```
curl -u user:bitnami http://192.168.1.126/projects.xml > projects.xml
```

In the above command the `curl` command is executed and the `>` `projects.xml` means, instead of writing the output to the console, write it to the file called `projects.xml`.

Amend the data in `projects.xml`

PUT the data back:

```
curl -u user:bitnami -X PUT -d @projects.xml \
http://192.168.1.126/projects.xml -i
```

In the above command I use:

- `-X` - specify the HTTP Verb, and I'm using PUT.
- `@projects.xml` means use the contents of `projects.xml` as the description.

That didn't work, so - try individual Project:

```
curl -u user:bitnami \
http://192.168.1.126/projects/17.xml > project.xml
```

Then try to PUT the individual Project back.

```
curl -u user:bitnami -X PUT -H "Content-Type: text/xml" \
-d @project.xml http://192.168.1.126/projects/17.xml \
-i --trace-ascii trace.txt
```

In the above command I use:

- `--trace-ascii` to generate more debug output for the request and have it written to the file `trace.txt`

At this point you have to conduct some experiments to see what you are allowed to include in the API message and what you are not.

For instance if you try and send back the full contents of `project.xml` you will trigger a 500 `Server Error` because you are trying to amend fields that you are not allowed to amend.

A quick look at the GUI will reveal that, on a Project, you are allowed to edit:

- Name
- Description
- Project Status
- default Context
- Default Tags
- Reviewed

The Project, written to `project.xml` looks like:

```
<?xml version="1.0" encoding="UTF-8"?>
<project>
  <id type="integer">17</id>
  <name>A New Projectaniheeiadtatd</name>
  <position type="integer">3</position>
  <description nil="true"/>
  <state>active</state>
  <created-at type="datetime">2015-01-12T11:48:12+00:00</created-at>
  <updated-at type="datetime">2015-01-12T11:48:12+00:00</updated-at>
  <default-context-id type="integer" nil="true"/>
  <completed-at type="dateTime" nil="true"/>
  <default-tags nil="true"/>
  <last-reviewed type="dateTime" nil="true"/>
  <not_done></not_done>
  <deferred></deferred>
  <pending></pending>
  <done></done>
</project>
```

I assumed that if I remove all the XML elements that do not relate to the above fields then I might be able to edit the Project.

So I removed:

```
<completed-at type="datetime" nil="true"/>
<created-at type="datetime">2015-01-12T11:48:12+00:00</created-at>
<id type="integer">17</id>
<position type="integer">3</position>
<updated-at type="datetime">2015-01-12T11:48:12+00:00</updated-at>
<not_done></not_done>
<deferred></deferred>
<pending></pending>
<done></done>
```

And I was able to amend the Project.

Without having used the GUI, I would have to experiment with the different fields, removing them from the message to see what I can edit and what I can't.

Deleting Data

Deleting is simply a matter of sending a DELETE message.

```
curl -u user:bitnami http://192.168.1.126/projects/1.xml -X DELETE
```

I use the:

- -X - option to specify the HTTP Verb as DELETE

Additional References

- Stack Overflow on reading a command for each line of a file
    - stackoverflow.com/questions/13939038[73]

Summary

From the command line, the API for Tracks makes it fairly easy to bulk load simple data.

Amending data is a little more problematic since I have to GET the XML details and then amend the XML to remove elements, as well as amend it for the data I want to change.

Deleting data is certainly simple with the API from the command line when using cURL.

I suspect that combining cURL with some simple Perl or Ruby might add additional value. cURL also provides us with a simple way of creating automated execution by calling it from batch or shell scripts.

I found that experimenting from the command line, and keeping my tool set as simple as possible allowed me to isolate any errors with my use of the API rather than thinking I might be using the tool incorrectly.

Since the API for Tracks is not documented in detail, in order to test it further I might want to:

- Read the source code,
    - github.com/TracksApp/tracks[74]
- Specifically the API code,
    - github.com/TracksApp/tracks/blob/master/config/routes.rb[75]
    - github.com/TracksApp/tracks/tree/master/app/controllers[76]

---

[73] http://stackoverflow.com/questions/13939038/how-do-you-run-a-command-for-each-line-of-a-file
[74] https://github.com/TracksApp/tracks
[75] https://github.com/TracksApp/tracks/blob/master/config/routes.rb
[76] https://github.com/TracksApp/tracks/tree/master/app/controllers

- Find any existing source that uses the API and see if I can crib hints and tips.

Interacting with an API manually is an important first step before trying to automate it. This allows us to explore the API calls and debug them in detail before coding them. We also learn a lot about the API as we explore.

Always remember that we can interact with any API, it is not just for programming, we need the flexibility to interact with the API manually if we are to fully test it.

cURL offers us one way of interacting, and it is a useful tool to master. It can often be easier to create a cURL command to document a repeatable API defect than to write code to trigger it.

Exploring the Tracks API with cURL Through a Proxy

Let it be known that I have a 'thing' for HTTP proxies.

I like to:

- Have the ability to observe the traffic that I'm using in my testing, both requests and responses.
- Have a record of the actual messages sent and responses received.
- Look back through these records later when I start writing code to automate the API to make sure that the requests I send with code are the same as those I sent when exploring the API.

You can find a video overview of using cURL through a proxy in the book support page videos:

- compendiumdev.co.uk/page/tracksrestsupport[77]

Using a Proxy with cURL

- `-x <proxydetails>` - use a proxy for HTTP requests e.g. e.g. `-x localhost:8080`
    - `--proxy <proxydetails>` - an alias for `-x`
- `-U <user:password>` - set the proxy username and password

If I want to repeat any of the commands I have issued, but send the requests through a proxy, all I have to do is add the `-x` and include my proxy details.

Since none of the proxies I have mentioned need a password (Fiddler, Charles, BurpSuite and OWASP ZAP) I can ignore the `-U` flag and just use `-x`

e.g.

---

[77] http://compendiumdev.co.uk/page.php?title=tracksrestsupport#vproxy

```
curl -x localhost:8080 \
    -u username:p4ssw0rd -H "Content-Type: text/xml" \
    http://192.168.17.129/contexts.xml
```

For Debugging

If I know the cURL commands work successfully, and I capture the actual requests sent when I issue the cURL commands, then I have a baseline set of 'good' requests.

If I then encounter problems when I automate, or use a REST client, then I can compare the messages sent by the new tools with the original cURL message requests.

If there are any differences between the new requests and those sent by cURL then the differences are a good place to start looking for a source of any problems.

The cURL messages are likely to be the most minimal messages that I send, i.e. fewer headers and request paraphernalia so they can act as a very simple baseline.

For Exploration

cURL can feel a little clumsy to repeat messages and amend the content of longer messages.

One benefit of playing them through a proxy is that we can then use the replay and edit functionality in the proxy to resend requests, and amend the requests to explore different conditions.

For Simple Scope Coverage

Some of the proxy tools, e.g. BurpSuite and OWASP ZAP, have 'fuzzers'. I can use a Fuzzer to iterate over values, in much the same way as I fed a file of values into the commands from Bash or the command line.

I can do the same from the 'fuzzers' in the Proxy tool GUI. I find it easier to use the Fuzzer GUI than use the command line to create lots of data.

Summary

Having the ability to feed tools through HTTP debug proxies offers us enormous flexibility in our testing.

We can store the requests and responses for future review or support evidence of testing.

We can resend edited requests from the proxy GUI as well as from cURL, this can make it easier to experiment with subtle tweaks for more in-depth testing or just until we learn how to make the request work.

We can review the requests and responses in an environment designed to render them, often with pretty printing and formatting.

The increased ability to observe, interrogate and manipulate the requests will increase your understanding of the API and flexibility in how you test the API.

cURL Summary

The official cURL web site - curl.haxx.se/docs[78]

For quotes - remember " on Unix means allow expansion of variables, so use ' on Unix and
" on Windows.

Examples:

- `curl <url>` - `GET` the URL
- `curl -X <verb> <url>` - issue the verb request to the URL e.g. `GET`, `PUT`, `POST` etc.
- `curl --version` - see what version you are using
- `curl "eviltester.com?p1=a&p2=b"` - `GET` a URL with parameters

Options:

- `-v` for verbose mode to see response
- `-i` for 'include' to see response headers
- `--trace <filename>` - output full message as a HEX and ASCII representation to the `<filename>`
- `--trace-ascii <filename>` - output full message trace as an ASCII representation to the `<filename>`
- `-b <set-cookie-line>` - sends the cookies e.g. `N1=V1;N2=V2`
- `-b <filename>` - when no = the file is read as cookies
- `-c <filename>` - writes any cookies to this cookie jar file
- `-H "<header>"` - sets the header e.g. `-H "Content-Type: application/json"`
- `-x <proxydetails>` - use a proxy for HTTP requests e.g. `localhost:8080`
- `--proxy <proxydetails>` - use a proxy for HTTP requests e.g. `localhost:8080`
- `U <user:password>` - set the proxy username and password
- `-A <user-agent>` - set the user agent
- `-o <file>` - send console output to a file

---

[78]http://curl.haxx.se/docs/

For PUT and POST payloads:

- `-d <data>` - send the data as form URL encoded
- `-d @<filename>` - sends data from a file (also `--data` etc.)
- `-F "name=@<filename>;type=text/plain"` - multi-part form data
- `-d "name=value"`

With `-d` options the Content Type is automatically set to:

- `application/x-www-form-urlencoded`

With `-F` options the Content Type is automatically set to:

- `multipart/form-data`

To split commands across multiple line use \ on Unix and ^ on Windows.
e.g. for Unix:

```
curl -u username:p4ssw0rd -H "Content-Type: text/xml" \
    http://192.168.17.129/contexts.xml
```

and for Windows:

```
curl -u username:p4ssw0rd -H "Content-Type: text/xml" ^
    http://192.168.17.129/contexts.xml
```

Exploring Tracks API with Postman REST Client

There are many REST Client GUIs available. I primarily use Postman.

- getpostman.com[79]

Postman is free and parts are Open Source. It was originally a Chrome Application and then converted into a Desktop Application.

This chapter will deal with the Desktop Application. Chrome Applications were deprecated in mid 2016 and will no longer be supported. I have moved the Chrome Application coverage to an appendix.

You can find a video overview of the Postman GUI on the book support page.

- compendiumdev.co.uk/page/tracksrestsupport[80]

The GUI

The Postman GUI is simple to use.

---

[79] https://www.getpostman.com/
[80] http://compendiumdev.co.uk/page/tracksrestsupport#vpostmangui

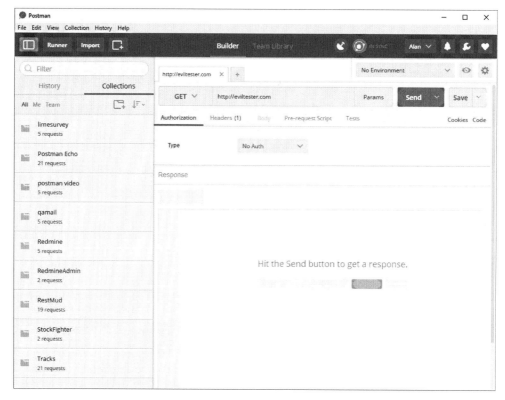

Postman GUI

- Central part of the screen is where we issue requests.
- Left hand side bar is a set of 'collections' of saved requests, and history of previous requests.

Issue Requests

We issue requests by amending the details in the main GUI.

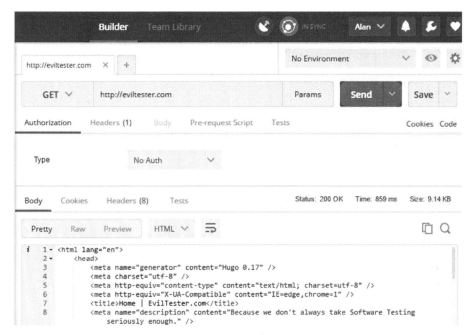

Issue a Request with Postman

We can change:

- The HTTP verb using the drop down. The screenshot shows a GET request but we can change that to any of the HTTP verbs e.g. POST, DELETE, PUT etc.
- The URL. The screenshot shows http://eviltester.com.
- The URL parameters by using the Params button, as this opens an easy way to edit any URL parameters.
- The Authorization used for Basic Auth, OAuth, etc.
- The Headers and add any header information we need.
- The Body if we are issuing a verb that allows body text e.g. POST.

Also:

- The Send button will issue the request.
- The Save button allows you to save the request to a Collection, use Save As if you are editing a request from a Collection.

After issuing a request the results will be shown in the Body tab and you can:

- See the HTTP Status code (in the above screenshot it was a 200 OK).
- See the time it took to receive the response.
- See the size of the response.
- View the message response as raw text.
- Pretty print the response.
- Change the type that Postman has rendered the response e.g. HTML, JSON etc. to use a different Pretty Print view.

You can also view any cookies issued, and the headers used.

What you can't see is the actual request sent - which is why I like to configure Postman to use a proxy server. (see explanation later)

The GUI is pretty straight forward for sending basic requests. If you explore you should figure it out. Assuming of course that you know the semantics of the HTTP requests you are sending.

Postman Collections

When you have a request that works in Postman you can save it to a Collection for re-use.

Postman can 'sync' Collections of requests to all devices. I find this useful since I often switch between working on a Windows machine, and on a Mac. Postman will sync the changes I made to the Collection on one machine with the other so I always have an up to date set of messages to use.

If you create a Postman account then you can share your Collections with others.

You can find the Postman Collection for this case study shared as:

- getpostman.com/collections/b9e81b009bfd21ec5e83[81]

I created a 'bit.ly' link in case you want to type it manually:

- bit.ly/2iPaxgj[82]

---

[81]https://www.getpostman.com/collections/b9e81b009bfd21ec5e83
[82]http://bit.ly/2iPaxgj

To use the Collection in Postman you would import it. Either use the "import" button or the drop down menu item on the "Collection" menu.

You can import the Collection using the link above with the "Import From Link" option, or from the file in the source code repository in the \postman folder.

Requests in Collections can be organized into folders to make them easier to use.

Environment Variables

Environment variables are very useful because they allow you to have a saved Collection of responses which you can send to multiple environments.

If I'm running Tracks in a virtual machine then the IP address of the virtual machine might change and I don't want to have to amend every request before I send it to use the most up to date IP address. Instead I would use environment variables in the request:

e.g. I would want to GET:

- `http://{{url}}/contexts.xml` rather than
- `http://129.128.1.16/contexts.xml`

The Environment variables GUI section are in the top right of the main builder part of the GUI:

Environment Management Section

This consists of:

- A drop down showing the list of environments.
- An 'eye' which shows the values of the environment variables.
- A settings 'cog' where you can manage the environments.

An environment is essentially a named set of key value pairs.

In order to use the Collection for this case study you would need to create an environment which had a url key value pair:

Environment Editing

Whatever key you create in the environment section, you can use in the requests with {{key}}.

e.g. if the key name was url you would write {{url}} in the request and it would be replaced by the value in the chosen environment.

If your requests fail, or you receive a result you don't expect, then make sure you check the environment variables exist and that they are set correctly.

Authentication

The Authentication tab lets you set a username and password for the authentication scheme used by the application.

You might need to amend this for the requests in the case study Collection. When you do, make sure you press the Update Request button prior to sending the request.

Using Postman Through a Proxy

To use Postman through a proxy, we have to start the application with a different command line argument.

```
Postman.exe --proxy-server=localhost:8888
```

You can find the location of Postman by looking at the shortcut created by the Postman installer.

After Postman has installed on Windows, I create a copy of the shortcut, edit the properties of the copied shortcut to add the command line arguments in the `Target` field.

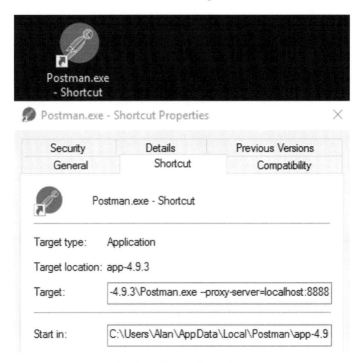

Postman Proxy Properties

You can find a video overview of using Postman through a proxy on the book support page.

- compendiumdev.co.uk/page/tracksrestsupport[83]

Proxy on Mac

To start a GUI application on Mac from the command line, you could use the `open` command from a terminal:

```
open /Applications/Postman.app --args --proxy-server=localhost:8888
```

The above command uses:

---

[83] http://compendiumdev.co.uk/page/tracksrestsupport#vpostmanproxy

- open to start the application
- /Applications/Postman.app which is the path of the Postman application
- --args to tell the open command to accept command line arguments
- --proxy-server=localhost:8888 the command line argument to set the proxy.

You can find other options for starting Mac applications from command line on this Superuser.com answer superuser.com/questions/16750[84]

Recreate cURL Requests in Postman

To start using Postman, the easiest thing to do is re-use the requests that you have been issuing from cURL.

Since you already know that the cURL request works, you can compare the cURL request with the Postman request to debug it.

If you are using a proxy then you can compare the sent request from both cURL and Postman, in detail, to spot any differences.

Summary

This chapter concentrated on the basics of the Postman desktop client and provided a simple overview of the GUI.

I fully expect this chapter to go out of date quickly, although I expect the basic functionality listed here to remain in Postman with much the same GUI.

The GUI isn't complicated, and if you experiment with it, you should be up and running with the basics very quickly.

To use the case study Collection, remember to create an 'environment' with a url and remember to change the Basic Auth values prior to sending a request. Or create an Admin user in your Tracks system with the username user which has a password of bitnami.

---

[84]https://superuser.com/questions/16750/how-can-i-run-an-application-with-command-line-arguments-in-mac-os

How to Use the Source Code

This chapter describes how to find the Java source code on GitHub, and how to load it into an IDE and run the data setup tests.

You may need to install the Java SDK and IDE - links are provided in this chapter for install instructions to help you use these tools.

You do not have to download the source code. The remainder of the book describes the code with excerpts taken from the source, but if you want to run the code against your own instance of Tracks, or amend it to experiment, then this chapter contains the information you can use to help you work with the source code.

Source Code Location

All of the source code for REST Assured and Java mentioned in the book is available on GitHub:

- github.com/eviltester/tracksrestcasestudy[85]

How to Use the Source Code

You can download the source code by visiting the releases and downloading one of the zip files:

e.g.

- github.com/eviltester/tracksrestcasestudy/releases[86]

Or use the 'Clone or download' button on the master code branch:

---

[85] https://github.com/eviltester/tracksrestcasestudy
[86] https://github.com/eviltester/tracksrestcasestudy/releases

- github.com/eviltester/tracksrestcasestudy[87]

You can clone the repository with Git, or download a zip of the current source.

If you know how to clone then you probably won't need any instructions on how to use the code, so the following instructions will use the zip download.

You will need to have installed:

- IntelliJ
- Java SDK
- Maven

If you want to run the code. You can find install instructions for these on my Java For Testers web site[88].

Download the zip from GitHub, and extract the contents of the zip file to a folder.

Load into IntelliJ

To load the code into IntelliJ

- Start IntelliJ.
- Choose 'File \ Open'.
- Select the folder that you extracted the downloaded code into, this folder should have the pom.xml file in it.
- The code should open in IntelliJ.

Changes to Make Prior to Running Any @Test

If you want to run any of the @Test methods then you should change the default values in the TestEnvDefaults.java file.

---

[87] https://github.com/eviltester/tracksrestcasestudy
[88] http://javafortesters.com/page/install/

```
public static final String theURL = "http://192.168.126.129";
public static final String adminUserName="user";
public static final String adminUserPassword="bitnami";
```

- `theUrl` should be the IP address of the machine that you have Tracks running on.
- `adminUserName` and `adminUserPassword` should match the values for your Tracks Admin user.

To Run an `@Test` Method

To run an `@Test` method:

- Open it in the code view window.
- 'right click' on the method name and select 'Run'.

To Find a Specific Class Mentioned in the Book

The book will mention the names of methods and classes. You will probably want to study the code in the IDE as well as in the book.

You can 'find' classes by pressing 'Ctrl+N' and typing the name of the class (on Mac use 'cmd+N').

For method names you can press 'Ctrl+Shift+Alt+N' to jump to them on Windows ('fn+cmd+N' on Mac).

These shortcuts are explained on the IntelliJ Web Site[89].

To Create Test Data in Tracks

To Create Test Data in Tracks:

- Make sure you amended the URL and user details in `TestEnvDefaults` class (find it using 'Ctrl+N' or 'cmd+N').
- Find the class `SetupTracksTestDataUtilityTest`.
- Right click on, and run, the method named `createTracksDataFromTestDataRetriever`.

---

[89]https://www.jetbrains.com/help/idea/2016.3/navigating-to-class-file-or-symbol-by-name.html

Summary

The source code to support this book, which you will see explained in the next few chapters is freely available to download on GitHub.

If you have trouble installing the IDE or Java SDK then watch the videos[90] linked to in this chapter as they walk you through install process step by step.

The remainder of the book describes the code using snippets taken from the GitHub source.

---

[90]http://javafortesters.com/page/install/

Starting to Automate

We have explored the API with cURL, proxies and Postman. Now we have a pretty good idea of how the API works and the type of responses it returns. We can start to think about automating it.

Why Explore First?

Part of the reason for doing the exploratory learning work first was to make sure we had several baselines to refer back to.

- cURL basic requests.
- Examples of the 'real' cURL requests and responses saved from the proxy.
- Saved requests in Postman with which we can quickly experiment.

Without the previous work, if something goes wrong when we automate we don't know if:

- We haven't understood the API.
- The API is broken.
- Our request is wrong.
- We are not receiving the correct responses.

But now we have evidence to compare back to if anything goes wrong. We can use the previous exploratory tools and approaches when we want to do something new in the GUI.

We have also built up basic coverage scenarios that we want to automate and now have a bit of a plan.

Choosing a Java Library

REST is essentially HTTP, so we could just use an HTTP library.

Using an HTTP library would be analogous to using cURL or the HTTP proxy. We gain a lot of low level configurable control, but it is a little slower and we work at the level of HTTP abstractions rather than REST requests.

Postman gives us a bit more of an abstraction on top of HTTP, since we can parse the responses more easily, but it is essentially an HTTP tool. The use of Collections is where the REST abstractions really start to come into play because we can organise the requests into a higher level set of categories.

There are always options when choosing a library for the programming language you will automate in.

For example in Java, a quick web search provided me with the following options:

- unirest.io[91]
- resty[92]
- jersey[93]
- JavaLite[94]
- REST Assured[95]
- OkHTTP[96]
- Apache HttpClient[97]

I chose to use REST Assured because I've used it before.

Although, really I'm cheating, because REST Assured uses Groovy, rather than Java, so adds some additional dependencies to the project that I don't really need.

But I have used REST Assured on a number of projects and it is pretty simple use. REST Assured also supplies some useful classes for parsing responses in XML and JSON.

In summary then, my decision to use the library is a pragmatic one based on previous experience. Not because it is the 'best' library. Not because I've evaluated them all and chosen the most suitable for the project. Instead, simply because I know I can create something quickly with it.

---

[91] http://unirest.io/java.html
[92] https://beders.github.io/Resty/Resty/Overview.html
[93] https://jersey.java.net/
[94] http://javalite.io/http
[95] https://github.com/rest-assured/rest-assured
[96] http://square.github.io/okhttp/
[97] https://hc.apache.org/

REST Assured Overview

REST Assured describes itself as a "Java DSL for simplifying testing of REST based services". I think 'DSL' is pushing it a bit far.

I think of REST Assured as a library, with a fluent interface, for automating REST services and HTTP applications easily.

All the examples for using REST Assured, use it as a set of `static` imports, which gives it the impression of looking more like a 'DSL' than a library.

I don't particularly like using lots of static imports, but since that is the convention for using REST Assured, that is what I will do.

You can find very good instructions for using REST Assured on the web site so I'm mainly going to describe how I used it, rather than all the features it provides.

The way that I use REST Assured is slightly different than the documentation describes and, I suspect, different from how many people use it. My usage differs because I don't really use the assertion mechanisms that REST Assured provides, or its BDD approach in the `@Test` methods.

Installation

Installation is very simple for Maven based projects - add the `rest-assured` dependency in the `pom.xml`.

- github.com/rest-assured/rest-assured/wiki/GettingStarted[98]

```
<dependency>
    <groupId>io.rest-assured</groupId>
    <artifactId>rest-assured</artifactId>
    <version>3.0.1</version>
</dependency>
```

Usage

I can use REST Assured to write `@Test` methods like the following:

---

[98] https://github.com/rest-assured/rest-assured/wiki/GettingStarted

```
@Test
public void aUserCanNotAccessIfNoBasicAuthHeaderUsingRestAssured(){

    given().
            contentType("text/xml").
    expect().
            statusCode(401).
    when().
            get("http://192.168.17.129/todos.xml");

}
```

Many older REST Assured examples are written in the given, expect, when style. And that is what I'm used to because I've used REST Assured before.

The interface for using REST Assured is very flexible and now the recommended style seems to be given, when, then, so I could equally have written:

```
@Test
public void aUserCanNotAccessIfNoBasicAuthHeaderUsingGivenWhenThen(){

    given().
            contentType("text/xml").
    when().
            get("http://192.168.17.129/todos.xml").
    then().
            statusCode(401);
}
```

You can see plenty of usage examples on the REST Assured web site:

- github.com/rest-assured/rest-assured/wiki/Usage[99]

I tend not to worry about which of those two conventions to use because I rarely use the REST Assured code in my actual @Test methods.

I use the REST Assured code in my lower level abstractions.

---

[99]https://github.com/rest-assured/rest-assured/wiki/Usage

Abstractions

I try to write code that is readable and is robust in the face of change.

It is possible to view the REST Assured library itself as providing a set of abstractions including:

- HTTP calls,
- Gherkin Given, When, Then,
- Assertions - e.g. in the form of `expect()`,
- JSON parsing,
- XML parsing,
- ...

Actually, that is quite a lot of abstractions.

It would be tempting to write all of my `@Test` methods using REST Assured, because then I get assertions, given, when & then, for free, and I don't have to worry about JSON parsing and ... etc.

However, if I have `@Test` methods which use the HTTP level abstractions then they will have to change when the API changes e.g. they call specific end points and use specific parameters. That approach would be suitable when I am specifically testing the structure of the API.

For example, if I have some end points on the API, and I want to check that each end point works, then this might be a valid abstraction level. I can mitigate some code changes by making endpoint URLs `String` constants.

Also, if I want to use the API to functionally test the application, and will be making multiple API calls in sequence, then I need to work at a level of abstraction above the HTTP endpoint calls.

In reality I want tests that look a little more like this:

```
@Test
public void aUserCanDeleteAProject(){

    TracksApi api = new TracksApi(TestEnvDefaults.getTestEnv());

    api.createProject("A New Project" +
                        new RandomDataGenerator().randomWord());
    Assert.assertEquals(201,
                        api.getLastResponse().getStatusCode());
    String projectId = new TracksResponseProcessor(
                                api.getLastResponse())
                                    .getIdFromLocation();

    // check we can get it
    api.getProject(projectId);
    Assert.assertEquals(200,
                        api.getLastResponse().getStatusCode());

    // check we can delete it
    api.deleteProject(projectId);
    Assert.assertEquals(200,
                        api.getLastResponse().getStatusCode());

    // check it has been deleted
    api.getProject(projectId);
    Assert.assertEquals(404,
                        api.getLastResponse().getStatusCode());
}
```

The above `@Test` method does use the REST Assured abstractions in the code - the `Response` class from REST Assured is used.

I have created a level of abstraction that maps on to the documented API i.e. `TracksApi` and this has methods which allow me to call the API and receive responses. Sometimes the responses are HTTP responses, sometimes they are domain objects. I always have access to the physical HTTP response via the `getLastResponse` method.

I assert in the `@Test`, but I don't use the REST Assured assertion mechanism, I use the `JUnit` assertions because these maintain a separation between the 'use' of the API, and the 'checking' or 'assertion' of the API results.

This means that if the physical structure of the API changes then my `@Test` code does not have to change, since the functionality that I'm using the API to test does not change. I will always be able to use the API to create, get, and delete Projects. The status code returned might change, but I doubt it.

The end point might change, and that won't impact my `@Test`, but it will require me to change other parts of the abstraction code. The data used to create the `Project` might change, but that probably won't require me to change the `@Test` since I don't really care what the details of the Project are, just that one is created.

This `@Test` isn't perfect.

- I could refactor this so that instead of sending the `createProject` method a 'name', I send it a `Project.newRandomProject()`.
- If the API were larger then having a single `TracksApi` with a long series of methods might not be readable or manageable, I might want to logically organise the API: `api.projects().get(id)` or `api.projects().delete(id)` etc.

But I don't worry about that now because I can amend the API abstractions over time.

Other Examples of REST Assured

I wanted to compare my use of REST Assured with other people so I used the search facility on github.com[100] to look for Java projects using the `rest-assured` library.

- GitHub search for Java projects using rest-assured[101]

I found the following projects which all use REST Assured directly in their `@Test` methods:

- github.com/testvagrant/RESTTests_RestAssured[102]
- github.com/OnBoardInformatics/WebMavenRestAssured[103]
- github.com/GSMADeveloper/RCS-REST-Tests[104]
  - This `GSMADeveloper` project is interesting because it imports the top level `RestAssured` class, rather than statically importing the `given` class. I found a few other personal projects doing this but haven't listed them as I thought one example would suffice.

---

[100] https://github.com

[101] https://github.com/search?l=Java&q=rest-assured&type=Repositories&utf8=%E2%9C%93

[102] https://github.com/testvagrant/RESTTests_RestAssured

[103] https://github.com/OnBoardInformatics/WebMavenRestAssured

[104] https://github.com/GSMADeveloper/RCS-REST-Tests

– I also have some examples using this style in the later JSON and XML processing chapter.

I found the following projects which adopted a similar approach to that used in this case study i.e. the use of abstractions on top of REST Assured which are used in the `@Test` methods:

- github.com/moolya-testing/rest-assured[105]

The basic criteria for choosing to list the projects here was that they looked like they were written by companies rather than individuals and they had enough code to make reading them interesting. I haven't included them because I think they are exemplars of how to write automated code. Their inclusion does not mean that I endorse them in any way. But I think it is useful to have examples to read.

REST Assured Related Reading

A quick web search revealed the following resources, if you want to learn more about REST Assured:

- Bas Djkstra's Open Source REST Assured Workshop[106]
  – Bas has open sourced a workshop that has basic REST Assured functionality for pre-emptive Basic Auth, REST Assured assertions, Oath2, POST, GET, URL Path parameters.
- Joe Colantonio has a few REST Assured blog posts written in a tutorial format:
  – Part 1 Getting Started[107]
  – Part 2 GET[108]
  – part 3 POST[109]
- Code examples on programcreek for REST Assured[110]
- Mark Winteringham has some REST Assured example code in his API Framework project on GitHub[111]

---

[105] https://github.com/moolya-testing/rest-assured
[106] http://www.ontestautomation.com/open-sourcing-my-workshop-an-experiment/
[107] https://www.joecolantonio.com/2014/02/07/rest-testing-with-java-getting-started-with-rest-assured/
[108] https://www.joecolantonio.com/2014/02/26/rest-testing-with-java-part-two-getting-started-with-rest-assured/
[109] https://www.joecolantonio.com/2014/04/24/rest-assured-how-to-post-a-json-request/
[110] http://www.programcreek.com/java-api-examples/index.php?api=com.jayway.restassured.RestAssured
[111] https://github.com/mwinteringham/api-framework

Summary

Try to explore the API interactively before you automate. This allows you to learn more about the API, and often allows you to experiment very quickly.

Prior to committing strategically to a library or tool, it is worth spending some time tactically automating the API to learn more and identify specific risk areas or problematic areas of the API.

As you automate, do keep thinking about the structure of the code and the abstractions you are using to make sure that you continually refactor to code that is maintainable and readable.

The Case Study Overview - Testing Tracks v 2.3.0

In this section I'll describe the work performed for the case study with version 2.3.0.

The version number is important. If you want to run the code and follow the steps exactly, then you should probably use the same version.

Remember, this is a case study, not a tutorial. This is time-bound and version-bound:

- *time-bound* - describing the decisions and approaches I took at a specific point in time, not guaranteed to be the 'best', but will be explained and justified.
- *version-bound* - guaranteed to work for a specific version.

You may well be working with a different version. You may very well be working with entirely different software in a different work environment so may choose to make different decisions.

The Tools

Just a quick reminder of the tools I'm using - I have already covered cURL and won't revisit it here.

For this documented case study I will be using:

- Java 1.8
- IntelliJ 2016.2.5
- Postman Desktop App v 4.9.3
- REST Assured v 3.0.1
- JUnit v 4.11

Originally I used:

- Java 1.7
- IntelliJ 2016.1.2
- Postman Chrome App v 4.2.0
- REST Assured v 2.9.0
- JUnit v 4.11

Different Tool Versions

I originally wrote the code with different tool versions.

I then decided to document the case study. At which point the tooling had updated so I updated my tools.

I did have to amend the code. If you use different versions then you might have to update the code. So I'm going to describe the type of changes you might have to make.

- Different Java Version,
    - no code changes, but in extreme circumstances you might have to amend the Java properties in IntelliJ.
- Different IntelliJ version,
    - no code changes, but the GUI might be different so screenshots might not match.
- Different Postman version,
    - no changes, but the GUI might not match.
- Different REST Assured,
    - when I upgraded from 2.9.0 to 3.1.0 the REST Assured team had changed their top level domain, so all imports broke.
        * I changed the `pom.xml` to import from `<groupId>io.rest-assured</groupId>` rather than `<groupId>com.jayway.restassured</groupId>`
        * This had a knock on effect on all the imports so I had to go through the code and change all imports.
        * This type of change does not happen often, so hopefully it will not happen again with REST Assured, and most of the code should work.
    - Some methods were deprecated
        * This is a fairly normal occurrence with libraries.
        * It might not impact your use of the code immediately because most libraries maintain backwards compatibility for a few versions when they deprecate code. But longer term you probably want to update the code to use the non-deprecated alternative, otherwise it might break in the future.

* In this upgrade, REST Assured deprecated the content method for setting the body of a POST and PUT method.
* Fortunately, because I use abstraction layers, I only had to change the putXmlMessageTo and postMessageTo methods in my HttpMessageSender class. If I had been using REST Assured at a lower level in the @Test code e.g. using given, when etc. in my @Test then I would likely have more changes to make.
* The change was simple and instead of using content I used body instead. The alternative method to use was described in the source code for the method and was visible when I used IntelliJ ctrl+Q JavaDoc view.

Code Location

For this section of the case study I will be exploring my use of Postman in combination with writing JUnit @Test methods which use REST Assured to make HTTP requests.

All Java code is available on GitHub[112], as is the Postman collection.

You can also access the Postman collection on-line:

- Postman collection on github[113]
- Shared Postman collection[114]
    - bit.ly/2iPaxgj[115]

The Approach

I approached the work of this case study with the following aims:

- Exploratory testing of the API with Postman.
- Automatically creating data to use with Exploratory Testing.
- Automating basic API functionality to support creating data and future testing.

I tended to jump back and forth between Postman, Code and the Tracks Web GUI to support investigation and results checking.

---

[112]https://github.com/eviltester/tracksrestcasestudy
[113]https://github.com/eviltester/tracksrestcasestudy/tree/master/postman
[114]https://www.getpostman.com/collections/b9e81b009bfd21ec5e83
[115]http://bit.ly/2iPaxgj

What I Automated

When working with Version 2.2.0 of Tracks, all I automated was the creation of random data into the Tracks system. I describe this in an appendix.

For version 2.3.0 I automated the creation of random data and users, and some @Test methods and abstractions to demonstrate using different parts of the API that required POST, GET, DELETE and PUT messages.

- Made it easier to configure proxy.
- Using new TracksApi(...),
    - Create (POST)
        * Context
        * Project
        * ToDo
        * user (had to bypass API to automate this)
    - Delete (DELETE)
        * Project
    - Amend (PUT)
        * Project
    - Read (GET)
        * Contexts
        * Project
        * Projects
        * TODO
        * ProjectTasks (TODOs)

Tracks v 2.2.0 and 2.3.0 have an interesting bug where you can create a user from the API, but you can't use that user to login and interact with the system.

So I had to simulate the form submission process that the GUI uses to create users. I call this approach "App as API" and I have a separate abstraction layer for this called TracksAppAsApi. This makes the case study more interesting because rather than just being a simple REST API interaction, you see how to combine the API with other automated approaches, which you will probably have to do in the real world when automating some systems.

- Via new TracksAppAsApi(...)
    - login

```
— createUser
```

I have tidied up the code a little to make it more readable, but I haven't performed a lot of refactoring on it. This means that the code isn't 'perfect' but it is 'usable'.

If I was to test Tracks a lot then I would refactor the code to improve it, and I describe some of the approaches for improving the code in a future chapter.

Summary

The case study covers two versions of Tracks. Version 2.2.0 is covered in an appendix and version 2.3.0 is covered in the main body of the book.

Version 2.2.0 to version 2.3.0 resulted in a few code changes because of package restructuring, but many of the code changes were isolated due to use of abstraction layers.

I had to work around a bug in the application in order to create users and this meant automating beneath the GUI, without using the API - an approach that I call "App as API".

The Case Study Creating Users with 'App as API'

One of the first things I have to do when automating an application is make sure that the data I need to support automated execution is in the system.

If it isn't in the system, I have to create it.

For Tracks, this means, creating a User, with some Projects and Tasks/TODOs with associated Contexts.

Creating a User In Tracks via the API

Fortunately, v 2.3.0 of Tracks has an API call to create Users.

A simple POST /users.xml

With the body content of:

```
<user>
  <login>username</login>
  <password>password</password>
</user>
```

This API exists i.e. it was in the documentation for version 2.2.0 and, although not documented for version 2.3.0, it is still present in the code, so can be called.

Unfortunately, the reason it is not documented for version 2.3.0 is that it has bugs.

It will create a User, but does not create all the referentially associated data to allow the User to be used or to login to the application.

Does This Mean We Have to Stop Automating Here?

We could create Users manually, and have them as static data in the system. The automated code could then rely on these users as static data and have them hard coded or stored in configuration files.

I much prefer to create the data I need, rather than rely on statically configured data in the application environment.

Sometimes it might not be possible to create the data:

- When creation takes too long.
- Overly complicated referential integrity makes it hard to inject data.
- The data has to be aged to support testing.

In the case of Tracks, we can create a User through the GUI, so perhaps we could automate through the GUI to create the User.

How to Create a User

Tracks is a Web Application, so I could use Selenium WebDriver to:

- start a browser,
- login as administrator,
- navigate to the User management,
- create a User.

All of this is perfectly feasible. It has the disadvantages that:

- We need another tool (Selenium WebDriver) in addition to our REST automating tool.
- It might slow down the test execution because starting and stopping browsers can take longer than REST API calls.
- It might require a different environment configuration to run the tests because now we need browsers installed.

If the rest of my automated execution was going to execute through the GUI then I might take this approach.

But, since we are targeting the REST API, I really want an approach that doesn't start browsers.

I could inject data into the database, but that means a dependency on ODBC drivers and potentially introducing referential integrity risks.

Instead I'm going to use a concept that I think of as "App as API".

'App as API'

"App as API" means treating the application as an API.

Sometimes this might mean using the GUI with WebDriver and writing the code so that it isn't obvious to the programmer that we are using the GUI e.g.

- `tracks.createUser("username", "password");`

I also use it to mean:

> **Instead of automating the GUI, automate what the GUI does.**

In Tracks, when you use the GUI to create Users, the GUI submits a form over HTTP to a particular URL on the server.

We could do that.

Risks:

- If the GUI changes, and the creation form is amended, then we have to change our code.
- It might be hard to simulate the GUI actions as HTTP requests.

If the GUI changes, we would have to change our code anyway. Because our other approach would involve automating the GUI.

It might be hard to simulate the GUI actions, so we will investigate the HTTP traffic triggered by the GUI to identify the appropriate message sequence and content.

Investigating How to Treat the APP as API

To investigate the HTTP traffic involved in creating a User:

- Use the GUI to create a User.
- Have all web traffic routed through an HTTP Debug Proxy like: Fiddler, OWASP ZAP, BurpSuite or Charles.
- Examine the HTTP requests involved in creating a User.
- Edit and resend the requests until I know the minimum set of requests to send.
- Edit and resend the requests until I know the minimum information needed in the requests.

What Requests Do I Need?

For Tracks, I discovered that I needed to:

- GET the /login page.
  - The form on the /login page contains a hidden input field called authenticity_-
    token, which I need to submit as part of the login request, otherwise I can't login.
- POST to the /login URL a form containing the Admin username, Admin password and
  authenticity_token from the GET request.
- POST a form to /users containing the username, password I wish to create and the
  admin user's authenticity_token.

As a general approach, I also keep a 'cookie jar' of the cookie values received in each response
and add that to each POST request. Unfortunately the authenticity_token is not set as a
cookie.

How Do We Do That?

In the supporting code base:

- src\test\java
- package api.version_2_3_0.trackstestdata
- class SetupTracksTestDataUtilityTest

The class SetupTracksTestDataUtilityTest is a utility @Test class. That means that I don't
tend to run it as a @Test I use it as a utility to create and configure an environment.

This @Test uses the TracksAppAsApi class to create Users.

The TracksAppAsApi class is the abstraction which implements sending of the appropriate
HTTP messages to the server.

I instantiate a TracksAppAsApi with a TestEnv object, which defines:

- The main environment URL.
- Admin username and password.
- If the environment is accessed through an HTTP proxy or not.

`TracksAppAsApi` has two public methods:

- `login`
- `createUser(String username, String password)`

And these are used as per the following example:

```
@Test
public void useTheAppAsAPIToCreateAUser(){
    TestEnv env = TestEnvDefaults.getTestEnv();
    TracksAppAsApi adminTracks = new TracksAppAsApi(env);

    adminTracks.login();
    adminTracks.createUser("bob99", "password66");
}
```

After running the above code, I could open up the system in a browser and login as bob99, or I could use the API with bob99.

TestEnvDefaults

Since this is fairly adhoc code, my `TestEnvDefaults` class is the main configuration point for my test code. If I want to run the tests on a different environment then I amend this class.

You can find `TestEnvDefaults` in the code:

- `src\test\java`
- `package api.version_2_3_0.environmentconfig`

The important points of note are the default configuration fields:

```
public static final String theURL = "http://192.168.126.129";
public static final String adminUserName="user";
public static final String adminUserPassword="bitnami";
public static final String proxyUrl="localhost";
public static final int proxyPort=8000;
```

- `theURL` is the IP address of the system reported in my virtual machine

- I used a VM from Bitnami so the default user was user with password bitnami
- I sometimes use a proxy to debug the messages, so that would be on localhost and I would amend the proxyPort to be the port the proxy is listening on.

Also, since these fields are all public static final the method getTestEnv creates a new TestEnv object using these values and returns it. Because setUserProxy(false) is used, the traffic is not diverted to a proxy:

```
public static TestEnv getTestEnv(){
    TestEnv env = new TestEnv(theURL, adminUserName, adminUserPassword);
    env.configureProxy(proxyUrl, proxyPort);
    env.setUseProxy(false);
    return env;
}
```

This TestEnv object can then be amended in the test if necessary. The TestEnvDefaults provides a central place for adhoc configuration.

> Note: Obvious future enhancements include overriding the hard coded values with environment variables or system properties.

TracksAppAsApi

The TracksAppAsApi exists in the main code folder structure:

- src\main\java
- package api.version_2_3_0.tracks

We can see from the constructor that the actual HTTP calls are made by an HttpMessage-Sender object:

```
public TracksAppAsApi(TestEnv env) {
    this.url = env.getURL();
    this.username = env.getUserName();
    this.password = env.getUserPassword();

    httpMessageSender = new HttpMessageSender(url);
    httpMessageSender.basicAuth(username, password);
    if(env.useProxy()){
        httpMessageSender.proxy(env.getProxyURL(), env.getProxyPort());
    }
}
```

The HttpMessageSender is the main class that uses RestAssured. Although use of RestAssured functionality has bled into other areas since I also use the XML parsing and Response object in the Tracks API abstractions.

I use Rest Assured slightly differently than the documentation, and other case studies for RestAssured that you might see, because I don't use the assertions and I only use its most basic features.

Login Via "App as API"

```
public void login() {

    Response response = httpMessageSender.getResponseFrom("/login");

    String authenticity_token =
                    getAuthenticityTokenFromResponse(response);

    // post the login form and get the cookies
    response = loginUserPost(username, password, authenticity_token);

    if(response.getStatusCode()==302) {
        //get the cookies
        loggedInCookieJar = response.getCookies();
    }else{
        System.out.println(response.asString());
        new RuntimeException("Could not login");
    }
}
```

Above code can be summarised as:

- Use the HttpMessageSender method to issue a GET request on the /login url.
- Parse the response to get the authenticity token.
- Post a form message using the authenticity token.
- Capture the cookies from the response as loggedInCookieJar to use in future messages.

And in more detail.

About HttpMessageSender

The HttpMessageSender GET request issues a GET on the /login url:

```
Response response = httpMessageSender.getResponseFrom("/login");
```

This is implemented using REST Assured in the HttpMessageSender as follows:

```
public Response getResponseFrom(String endpoint){
    return getResponseFrom(endpoint, anEmptyCookieJar() );
}

public Response getResponseFrom(String endpoint,
                            Map<String, String> cookieJar) {

    URL theEndPointUrl = createEndPointURL(url, endpoint);

    String ct = "text/html,application/xhtml+xml," +
                "application/xml;q=0.9,*/*;q=0.8";

    Response ret =
            given().
                auth().preemptive().
                        basic(authUser, authPassword).
                cookies(cookieJar).
                contentType(ct).
            get(theEndPointUrl.toExternalForm()).
            andReturn();

    return setLastResponse(ret);
}
```

In one respect I'm *just* using RestAssured as a simple and easy to use HTTP library. But really, I'm adding abstraction layers to the code to make each class readable and maintainable for the domain that it targets.

- HttpMessageSender works at the HTTP domain and sends HTTP messages.
  - But... this isn't completely true since it is HTTP messages specifically for the Tracks application.
  - Hence the reason why you can see the contentType has been configured to xml, because the Tracks API uses XML.

Other points to note:

- I pass in the cookie jar that I'm building up across different messages. And this is just a simple Map.
- I don't use any of the REST Assured assertions because I'm using REST Assured to construct and send HTTP messages.
- I store the response as lastResponse so that I can retrieve it if I need to.
- The method returns a Response which is a RestAssured object. This means that I haven't isolated REST Assured to *just* the HTTP messages, I also use it in the TrackAppAsApi and TracksApi.
- The Basic Auth message header is configured in the messages with
  - auth().preemptive().basic(authUser, authPassword)
  - preemptive means that only one request is sent to the server, if you take this out then you'll see multiple messages are sent when a request is made.

You can find out more about the *pre-emptive* and *challenge* modes for Basic Authentication on the REST Assured website.

- github.com/rest-assured/rest-assured/wiki/usage#preemptive-basic-authentication[116]

Parsing the Response in the login to Extract Token

Now that we know how the message is sent, we have to examine the response and extract the authenticity token.

If I look at an extract of the contents of the response body:

response.body().asString()

The login form in the response looks a bit like this:

---

[116]https://github.com/rest-assured/rest-assured/wiki/usage#preemptive-basic-authentication

```html
<h3>Please log in to use Tracks:</h3>
<div id="database_auth_form" style="display:block">
    <form accept-charset="UTF-8" action="/login" method="post">
        <div style="display:none">
            <input name="utf8" type="hidden" value="&#x2713;" />
            <input name="authenticity_token" type="hidden"
                value="GVnfu2oUd6HvhXf2bEJSf17U2M0n/TwKZu925E97nuQ=" />
        </div>
      <table>
      <tr>
        <td>
          <label for="user_login">Login:</label>
        </td>
        <td>
          <input type="text" name="user_login" id="user_login"
                 value="" class="login_text" />
        </td>
      </tr>
. . .
```

And you can see the authenticity_token is present as a hidden field.

We want to extract that value so that we can pass it in with our HTTP message.

I extract it using the XmlPath functionality from REST Assured. Which requires me to use Groovy's GPath syntax for a query.

```java
private String getAuthenticityTokenFromResponse(
                                    Response response){
    // get the authenticity_token from the response
    XmlPath htmlParser = response.body().htmlPath();
    String auth_token_path =
            "**.find {it.@name =='authenticity_token'}.@value";
    String authenticity_token = htmlParser.get(auth_token_path);
    return authenticity_token;
}
```

This query basically says:

- **.find - search all nodes for...
- {it.@name =='authenticity_token'} - elements with a name attribute with the text authenticity_token

- `.@value` - and return the value attribute

I found this syntax quite hard to use initially and it took me some time to find helpful documentation.

Eventually I used a combination of the REST Assured documentation, GPath documentation and StackOverflow to build the query.

- github.com/rest-assured/rest-assured/wiki/usage#xml-using-xmlpath[117]
- blog.jayway.com/2013/04/12/whats-new-in-rest-assured-1-8/[118]
- hascode.com/2011/10/
    - testing-restful-web-services-made-easy-using-the-rest-assured-framework[119]
- stackoverflow.com/questions/2117739/
    - what-is-the-full-syntax-of-groovys-gpath-expressions[120]

Sending the `login` Form

```
response = loginUserPost(username, password, authenticity_token);
```

The `TracksAppAsApi` class `login` method sends the login form by calling the following private method called `loginUserPost`. This method uses the `authenticity_token` that we extracted from the page returned in the previous HTTP request.

```
private Response loginUserPost(String username, String password,
                              String authenticityToken) {

    UrlParams params = new UrlParams();
    params.add("utf8","%E2%9C%93");
    params.addEncoded("authenticity_token",
                      authenticityToken);
    params.add("user_login", username);
    params.add("user_password", password);
    params.add("user_noexpiry", "on");
    params.add("login", "Sign+in");
```

[117] https://github.com/rest-assured/rest-assured/wiki/usage#xml-using-xmlpath
[118] https://blog.jayway.com/2013/04/12/whats-new-in-rest-assured-1-8/
[119] http://www.hascode.com/2011/10/testing-restful-web-services-made-easy-using-the-rest-assured-framework/
[120] http://stackoverflow.com/questions/2117739/what-is-the-full-syntax-of-groovys-gpath-expressions

```
        Response response = httpMessageSender.postFormMessageTo(
                                              params.toString(),
                                  "/login");
        return response;
    }
```

You can see that I'm using a `UrlParams` class that I created to make it easier to build up a String of parameters without having to encode them or add "&" between all the parameters.

This calls the `HttpMessageSender` method `postFormMessageTo` to post the form to the `'/login'` end point.

The `postFormMessageTo` methods call the `postMessageTo` method but set the `contentType` header to a form submission `"application/x-www-form-urlencoded"`

```
    public Response postFormMessageTo(String msg, String endpoint){
        return postFormMessageTo(msg, endpoint, anEmptyCookieJar());
    }

    public Response postFormMessageTo(String msg, String endpoint,
                                Map<String, String> cookieJar){
        return postMessageTo(msg, endpoint,
                "application/x-www-form-urlencoded", cookieJar);
    }
```

And the `postMessageTo` method sends the actual HTTP message:

```
    private Response postMessageTo(String msg, String endpoint,
                                String contentType,
                                Map<String, String> cookieJar){

        URL theEndPointUrl = createEndPointURL(url, endpoint);

        Response ret =
                given().
                        auth().preemptive().
                            basic(authUser, authPassword).
                        body(msg).
                        contentType(contentType).
                        cookies(cookieJar).
                when().
```

```
                    post(theEndPointUrl.toExternalForm()).
          andReturn();

  // ignore CREATED UNAUTHORIZED CONFLICT
  if( ret.statusCode()!=201 && ret.statusCode()!=401 &&
      ret.statusCode()!=409 ){
      System.out.println("POTENTIAL BUG - " +
                         ret.statusCode() + " FOR " +
                         endpoint + "\n" + msg );
  }

  return setLastResponse(ret);
}
```

- Using RestAssured as an HTTP library.
- preemptive Basic Authentication is used.
- A cookie jar is used to maintain a session across HTTP messages.
- I have coded a warning to alert me for the presence of any potential bugs or unexpected response codes, to support my monitoring and testing.
- The response is maintained as lastResponse.

Maintaining the Session

The final part of the login process is to capture the session cookies that represent the session:

```
if(response.getStatusCode()==302) {
    //get the cookies
    loggedInCookieJar = response.getCookies();
}else{
    System.out.println(response.asString());
    new RuntimeException("Could not login");
}
```

All I do at this point is ensure that the response from posting the login form is a 302 redirect, because when using the GUI we are redirected to the appropriate page. For "App as API" I care that we receive the redirect and I care about the session cookies that are returned.

If I don't get the 302 then I throw a RuntimeException. This will fail any @Test method. But it isn't an assertion, it is an Exception because we are only logged in if the 302 is returned.

I make it a RuntimeException rather than a checked exception because I don't want to force all client code of the TracksAppAsApi to handle that exception.

It doesn't matter which cookies are returned. I store the entire Map of cookies in the response, and I send that Map of cookies with any future "App as API" HTTP message.

Create a User

The TracksAppAsApi class has the createUser method which sends the two HTTP messages required to create a User in the system.

```java
public Response createUser(String username, String password){

    Response response= httpMessageSender.getResponseFrom(
                                        "/signup",
                                        loggedInCookieJar);

    String authenticity_token =
                    getAuthenticityTokenFromResponse(response);

    // cookies seem to change after signup
    // - if I don't use these then the request fails
    loggedInCookieJar = response.getCookies();

    response =  createUserPost(username, password,
                              authenticity_token,
                              loggedInCookieJar);

    if(response.getStatusCode()!=302) {
        //get the cookies
        loggedInCookieJar = response.getCookies();
    }else{
        System.out.println(response.asString());
        new RuntimeException(
                String.format("Could not create user %s %s",
                                    username, password));
    }

    return response;
}
```

The above has the same format as the login process.

- First we have to GET the page with the form, the /signup page, and we use the cookie jar which has our logged in session cookie.
- The authenticity_token is extracted from the response because this is a new token embedded in the form for this create request.
- I also have to re-capture the cookies between requests.
- I then 'POST' the simulated 'create User form' and capture the cookies.

You can see in the comments in the method that I had to refresh the cookies in the cookie jar after visiting the /signup page. I learned this the hard way through having to debug why signup was failing.

This was the first system where I had to do this. I didn't spend a lot of time investigating 'why' this happened. Because at this point I'm modelling how the application actually works, rather than if it is supposed to work this way. Normally I don't have to refresh session cookies during the use of the application.

The actual 'Create User form' uses the same process as login:

```
private Response createUserPost(String username, String password,
                                String authenticityToken,
                                Map<String, String> loggedInCookieJar) {

    UrlParams params = new UrlParams();
    params.add("utf8","%E2%9C%93");
    params.addEncoded("authenticity_token", authenticityToken);
    params.add("user%5Blogin%5D", username);
    params.add("user%5Bpassword%5D", password);
    params.add("user%5Bpassword_confirmation%5D", password);

    Response response = httpMessageSender.postFormMessageTo(
                                        params.toString(),
                                        "/users",
                                        loggedInCookieJar);


    return response;
}
```

Summary

That's the basic process, and you've seen a pretty good example of "App as API".

I had to do this out of necessity because of a bug in the system, and I didn't want the overhead of automating the GUI.

So instead we automate what the GUI does.

- Automate the minimum set of requests that the GUI issues.
- Replicate the minimum headers and form parameters.
- We know what these are because we explored the GUI interactively through a proxy.
- The form parameters and data are copied from the proxied requests.
- We don't question if this is 'right' or 'wrong', we model what we 'need' to do to get it working.
- Put some checks in place as `RuntimeException` to enforce the promised contract from the method name e.g. `login`, `createUser`.
- The HTTP message implementation is delegated to `RestAssured`.

To see the full code in context, you should look at:

- `src\test\java`
    - package `api.version_2_3_0.tracksapi`
        * class `AuthenticationTest`
            · `aUserCanAuthenticateAndUseAPIWithBasicAuth`
- `src\main\java`
    - package `api.version_2_3_0.tracks`
        * class `TracksAppAsApi`
            · `login`
            · `createUser`
    - package `api.version_2_3_0.tracks.http`
        * class `UrlParams`
        * class `HttpMessageSender`

The Case Study - Create Random Users Utility `@Test`

When I was writing the code for this case study and testing Tracks. I needed to create a bunch of users in the system for exploratory and performance testing.

Generally for a test approach involving a lot of automating, I will create users as required during the automated execution. But for the scenarios above, I will often batch create users in advance.

If I'm teaching a class on exploratory testing, from which a lot of this code derives, then I will certainly create users in advance so that students can dive straight into the system.

The code for this chapter can be found in:

- `src\test\java`
- `package api.version_2_3_0.trackstestdata`
- `class SetupTracksTestDataUtilityTest`

A Utility `@Test` Case

I often write `@Test` methods which are utilities, rather than part of my automated coverage suite.

By this I mean that:

- I write a method annotated with `@Test`.
- I `@Ignore` the method so it doesn't run automatically.
- I right click and run the `@Test` from the IDE to 'do something'.

In effect, the `@Test` method is there to support my testing. e.g. the full code for the earlier `@Test` method for creating a user:

```
@Ignore("Do not run this tests automatically, " +
        "this is a utility to create a user in the system")
@Test
public void useTheAppAsAPIToCreateAUser(){
    TestEnv env = TestEnvDefaults.getTestEnv();
    TracksAppAsApi adminTracks = new TracksAppAsApi(env);

    adminTracks.login();
    adminTracks.createUser("bob99", "password66");
}
```

You saw the above code earlier, but now you can see that it has an `@Ignore` annotation.

- I use this `@Test` as a utility to create a single user in the system.
- I amend the username and password before executing it.
- I execute it by right clicking on it in the IDE and running as a Unit test.

This approach allows me to:

- Create simple utilities very quickly.
- Create utilities without worrying about a user interface.
- Use all my test abstractions without compiling and extracting to different `.jar`.
- Have no need to create a manifest file and `main` methods.
- Work directly from the IDE and the version controlled code.

The Main Utility `@Test` Method

I have a more complicated, or larger, utility `@Test` method for creating users in the system, which I'll describe in this section.

The main test is as follows and uses a combination of API abstractions, "App as API" abstractions, and local abstractions:

```
@Ignore("Do not run these tests automatically," +
        "they are not 'tests', they help me work")
@Test
public void createTracksDataFromTestDataRetriever()
                                    throws MalformedURLException {

    TestEnv env = TestEnvDefaults.getTestEnv();
    TestDataRetriever testData = new RandomFoodBackedDataRetriever();
    TracksAppAsApi adminTracksUserAppSession = new TracksAppAsApi(env);

    // in version 2.3.0 of tracks the basic auth does
    // not work for creating a user through the GUI
    // needed a more complicated app as API process
    adminTracksUserAppSession.login();

    // create the users name password map
    Map<String,String> usersNamePassword = new HashMap<String, String>();
    // add the admin user
    usersNamePassword.put(env.getUserName(), env.getUserPassword());

    generateUserNameAndPasswordList(usersNamePassword,
                                    newUserPattern,
                                    newPasswordPattern);

    createUsersViaAppAndApi(env, adminTracksUserAppSession,
                            theContexts, usersNamePassword);

    createProjectsForUsers(env, testData, usersNamePassword);
}
```

As a high level explanation:

- Use the default test environment,
  - this has usually been configured for the automated test code so 'should' work,
  - if I want to conduct more adhoc testing on a different environment then I could create a TestEnv here with the details I need.
- Create a random data generator - I'll explain this in an appendix, but this one is 'food based'.
- Create a Tracks "App as API" for creating users.
- Login to the "App as API" session.
- Randomly generate a Map of usernames and passwords that I will create.

- Create the list of users.
- Create Projects with data for each of the users randomly.

There is nothing clever about the above code. Originally it was written as a single long method and I refactored code blocks to local methods to make the test readable. This means that I essentially have a local abstraction layer which is only used by the utility @Test e.g. createUsersViaAppAndApi.

Configuring the @Test User Creation Utility

Because this is a utility class, and it doesn't really have a GUI, I make the configuration options very obvious as fields at the head of the class. Even if these options are only used in one supporting private method, I'll make them fields so it is easy for me to amend and configure my utility.

```
private final int MAX_NUMBER_OF_TODOS=20;

// Max number of projects to create
// -ve to use the number of projects
// from the testdata generator
private int numberOfProjectsLimit = 10;

// Number of users not enabled
// for 0 users, the default username password will be used for all
// for more than one user, the users will be created
// then for each project a random user will be used for each project
private int numberOfUsersToUse = 30;

// Username and Password patterns
private final String newUserPattern = "nuuser%d";
private final String newPasswordPattern = "bitnami%d";

// Contexts to create
private String[] theContexts = {"work", "home",
                                "shopping", "schoolrun"};
```

- MAX_NUMBER_OF_TODOS when I randomly generate TODO items for Projects I will create a maximum of 'this' many.

- numberOfProjectsLimit when I randomly create Projects for a user, I will create maximum of 'this' many.
- numberOfUsersToUse the number of users to create.
- newUserPattern and newPasswordPattern are the patterns I will use to create users.
  - The %d is replaced with a number from 1 to numberOfUsersToUse.
  - If the patterns were user%d and password%d then we would generate: (user1, password1), (user2, password2) etc.
  - I usually amend these prior to running the utility, just in case I have run it before in this environment to avoid a username clash.
- theContexts is an array of values to use for GTD context e.g. tags for 'where I might do a TODO' these are hard coded to make the data more 'realistic'. The code is designed to work with whatever length of array so I can easily add more Contexts if I want to when generating data.

Local Abstractions Overview

Generate Username and Password List

```
private void generateUserNameAndPasswordList(
                        Map<String, String> usersNamePassword,
                        String userNamePattern, String passwordPattern) {

    for(int userNumber=1; userNumber<numberOfUsersToUse; userNumber++){
        String newUsername = String.format(userNamePattern, userNumber);
        String newPassword = String.format(passwordPattern, userNumber);
        usersNamePassword.put(newUsername, newPassword);
    }
}
```

I create a Map of all the users I am going to create in advance.

This allows me to later, iterate over, the items in the Map or randomly select users from the Map.

I use the username as the Key to avoid duplicates.

This simply uses the String.format to create a string where the %d in the pattern is replaced with the userNumber from the for loop.

Create Users with Contexts

Each user in Tracks needs to have Contexts configured to allow it to create TODO lists.
e.g. when I am at work I will tidy my desk, where work is the Context.

```
private void createUsersViaAppAndApi(TestEnv env,
                                     TracksAppAsApi adminTracksUserAppSession,
                                     String[] contexts,
                                     Map<String, String> usersNamePassword) {

    // create the users - ignores duplicates
    for(String aUserName : usersNamePassword.keySet()){

        // create a user
        String aPassword = usersNamePassword.get(aUserName);
        adminTracksUserAppSession.createUser(aUserName, aPassword);
        createContextsForUser(env, contexts, aUserName, aPassword);
    }
}
```

The above code works as follows:

- For every user in the Map,
    - create the user using the "App as API",
    - create all the Contexts for the user.

The local abstraction method createContextsForUser uses the normal Tracks API to create
the Context for a user. I will explain the TracksApi in a future chapter.

```
private void createContextsForUser(TestEnv env, String[] contexts,
                                   String aUserName, String aPassword) {
    // create the contexts for the user
    for(String aContext : contexts){

        // each user needs to create their own context
        TracksApi normalTracksUser = new TracksApi( env.getURL(),
                                                    aUserName, aPassword);

        Response response = normalTracksUser.createContext(aContext);
```

```
if(response.getStatusCode()==201 || response.getStatusCode()==409){
    // 201 - Created
    // 409 - Already exists
}else{
    System.out.println( "Warning: Creating Context " + aContext +
                        " Status Code " + response.getStatusCode());
}
    }
}
```

The above code also checks the status code returned for the API call to `createContext`. It ignores 'created' and 'already exists' status codes, but in the event that something else happens, it outputs a warning to the console.

Having console output like this is useful for a 'utility' `@Test` because it is being run interactively by the user, so they can monitor the console output to see if there are any issues.

If this were to be a fully automated process then we would want to make this logging approach more formal and possibly throw an exception and stop the creation process if we couldn't create a user.

Create Projects for the Users

The remainder of the code in this class creates Projects for the users.

This is only complicated because of the referential integrity involved and because we want to randomise the data enough to make it readable and understandable for a user to interact with.

The referential integrity requires that:

- A user exists.
- A user has Contexts.
- Projects are created for an existing user.
- TODOs are created for a Project and have a Context associated with them.

```java
private void createProjectsForUsers(TestEnv env, TestDataRetriever testData,
                                    Map<String, String> usersNamePassword) {
    RandomDataGenerator wordGenerator = new RandomDataGenerator();

    List<Project> projects = testData.getProjects();

    // LOOP: create a project
    for( Project aProject : projects) {

        // Chose a random user
        String randomUserName = selectRandomUserName(usersNamePassword.keySet());
        String theRandomUsersPassword = usersNamePassword.get(randomUserName);

        TracksApi normalTracksUser = new TracksApi( env.getURL(),
                                                    randomUserName,
                                                    theRandomUsersPassword);

        List<TracksContext> contextList = normalTracksUser.getContexts();

        String projectId = createProjectViaAPIForUser(
                                    wordGenerator, aProject,
                                    normalTracksUser);

        if(projectId!=null){
            List<Todo> todos = testData.getTodosForProject(projectId);
            createRandomNumberOfTodosInProjectForUser(
                                    wordGenerator,
                                    normalTracksUser,
                                    contextList, projectId,
                                    todos);
        }

        numberOfProjectsLimit--;
        if(numberOfProjectsLimit==0){
            break;
        }
    }
}
```

The above code:

- Creates a random data generator to use when creating Project names and TODOs.

- `getProjects` randomly generates a list of Projects.
- For each of the Projects (or until we have reached our `numberOfProjectsLimit`),
    - randomly select a user we created earlier,
    - create an API connection for that user,
    - create a random Project for that user using the API,
    - if we created the Project successfully then
        * use the API to create a random number of TODOs in the Project.

Again, this code was written as a block, then refactored using 'extract to method' to make the code readable and more maintainable.

Select a User

```
private String selectRandomUserName(Set<String> userNames){
    String[] names  = userNames.toArray(new String[userNames.size()]);
    return names[new Random().nextInt(names.length)];
}
```

The `selectRandomUserName` method has a pretty obvious function:

- Given a `Set` of `Strings` convert it to an array.
- Select a random item from the array.

I mention it because it provides a very simple example of having used 'refactor to method'.

Originally, the two lines in the method would have been in the `createProjectsForUsers` method as:

```
String[] names  = usersNamePassword.keySet().toArray(
                                new String[usersNamePassword.
                                            keySet().size()]);
String randomUserName =  names[new Random().nextInt(names.length)];
```

But, the code above seemed a little hard to read.

Rather than add a lot of comments into the code, I highlight the two lines and right click to use the IntelliJ refactoring tool - 'refactor to method'.

This keeps the code simpler and easier to maintain.

Create a Project Via API

We use the Tracks API to create a Project, then capture the `id` to use in future API calls.

```java
private String createProjectViaAPIForUser(
                                RandomDataGenerator wordGenerator,
                                Project aProject,
                                TracksApi normalTracksUser) {

    String newProjectName = aProject.name() + " " +
                            wordGenerator.randomWord();
    System.out.println(newProjectName);

    Response response = normalTracksUser.createProject(newProjectName);

    String projectId = null;

    if(response.statusCode()==201) {
        projectId = new TracksResponseProcessor(response).
                                    getIdFromLocation();
    }
    return projectId;
}
```

The code is pretty simple:

- Create a random Project name.
- Call the `createProject` API call to create it.
- If the response is a `201` (created) then capture the `id` (from the `location` header).
- Finally, return `projectId` for future use.

The method `createProjectViaAPIForUser` is the type of method that could easily be moved into a more widely shared abstraction layer since it processes the response of the message to retrieve an `id` from the `location` header in the response message.

The code above introduces us to another class in the API code. The `TracksResponsePro-cessor`, this would grow to become a home for any extract methods that process the HTTP message responses from Tracks. We will look at the actual API abstractions later.

Hopefully you can see the point of the API abstractions. The `@Test` is not cluttered with the REST Assured `Given When Then` notation, instead we have an instantiated `TracksApi` object called `normalTracksUser` and we have methods which call the API e.g. `createProject`, `getContexts` etc. All of which makes our `@Test` code more readable and maintainable.

Create ToDo Items for Project

The final step in creating a Project is to add some TODO items to the Project. Which we do by randomly choosing a number of TODO items to add, then looping around until we have created all the TODOs.

```
private void createRandomNumberOfTodosInProjectForUser(
                                    RandomDataGenerator wordGenerator,
                                    TracksApi normalTracksUser,
                                    List<TracksContext> contextList,
                                    String projectId,
                                    List<Todo> todos) {
    // LOOP: generate a random number of todos
    int numberOfTodos = new Random().nextInt(MAX_NUMBER_OF_TODOS);

    while (numberOfTodos > 0) {
        // randomly choose a context
        TracksContext rndcontext = contextList.get(
                                    new Random().
                                        nextInt(contextList.size()));

        // randomly choose a todo name
        Todo rndtodo = todos.get(new Random().nextInt(todos.size()));

        // add the todo to the project and a context
        normalTracksUser.createTodo(rndtodo.name() + " " +
                                wordGenerator.randomWord(),
                                projectId, rndcontext.id());

        if(normalTracksUser.getLastResponse().getStatusCode()!=201){
            System.out.println("Warning: Possible error creating Todo " +
                            normalTracksUser.getLastResponse().
                                        getStatusCode());
        }

        numberOfTodos--;
    }
}
```

- Randomly generate a `numberOfTodos` to create, but no more than `MAX_NUMBER_OF_-TODOS`.
- Choose a random Context to add to the TODO.

- Randomly choose one of the TODO names we generated earlier.
- Use the API to `createTodo` for the Project with an extra random word on the TODO text.
- For general debugging use, if we don't receive a `201` response then warn the user by writing information to the console.

Summary

And with that, you have seen the main `@Test` utility class which uses the API abstractions and "App as API" abstractions.

This demonstrates that abstraction code:

- can be very readable,
- is more readable than REST Assured calls directly,
- is not just for 'testing' we can also use it for creating helpful utilities.

Also you've seen that:

- `@Test` can be used for writing adhoc utility code.
- `@Ignore` prevents `@Test` code running automatically, but still allows us to run code from the IDE.
- We can combine "App as API" and "API" code when the abstractions exist, and still have readable code.

The Case Study - API Abstraction

You have seen the API Abstractions used as part of the 'create user' @Test utility.

In this chapter we will explore them in more detail.

Overview of the API Abstractions

Most of the API abstractions are in src\main\java.

They are in the main folder path because they are not test code.

In this case study the abstractions are primarily used to support testing, but they are not @Test code. They are library code which makes it easy to use the API.

You can find the API code root in:

- src\main\java
- package api.version_2_3_0.tracks;

Multiple Versions

I don't normally add the version number into the package but the case study code has been built up over two different versions of Tracks and is example code, so I have retained the previous versions to support comparison and evolution of the code.

Normally my versioning would be managed by version control.

Although I might encounter a situation like this on a production project e.g. if I had to automate multiple versions of the API - but I suspect if this were the case I might try and split the API code into its own project and use dependency management to control which version of the API code I use.

Classes

The main classes that make up the API Abstraction are:

- `TracksApi` the main class that I use to access the API calls.
- `TracksApiEndPoints` a class to generate URLs for accessing the Tracks API calls.
- `TracksAppAsApi` this isn't officially API but I have added it in the same package structure. In a more production oriented project I might have chosen to more clearly partition the API library code from this "App as API" code.
- `TestEnv` represents the environment configuration details - URL, Admin user, proxy.

We also have `http` and `entity` classes:

- `package api.version_2_3_0.tracks.http`
- `package api.version_2_3_0.tracks.entity`

The `http` classes are the lower level classes which deal with the `http` message concerns:

- `HttpMessageSender` implementation of HTTP messages.
- `UrlParams` class to control creation of a list of URL Parameters.
- `URLifier` a simple utility to convert a string to a `URL`.

The `entity` classes represent API level Tracks objects:

- `TracksContext`
- `TracksProject`
- `TracksTodo`

We also have a class called `TestEnv`. This is not in the `tracks` hierarchy because it is more generic, but could easily be moved into the `tracks` hierarchy given that this code only automates the Tracks application.

Interacting with the API

The methods in `TestApi` relate to sending messages to the API.

Currently the `TestApi` supports:

- `createContext` to create a Context.
- `createProject` to create a Project.
- `createTodo` to create a TODO for a Project and Context.
- `getContexts` to return all the Contexts for the current user, this is returned as a `List` of Contexts as domain objects i.e. `TracksContext`.
- `getProjects` to return a `List` of Projects as domain objects i.e. `TracksProject`.
- `getProject` to return a specific Project as `TracksProject`.
- `getProjectTasks` to return a `List` of the TODOs for a specific Project as domain objects i.e. `TracksTodo`.
- `getTodo` to return a specific TODO from Tracks as a `TracksTodo`.
- `amendProject` to amend specific fields on a Project.
- `deleteProject` to delete a specific Project.
- `getLastResponse` to return the 'last response' received by the HTTP layer.

Also:

- `createUserAPI` to create a user via the API, is listed but marked as `@Deprecated` because we have to use "App as API" instead.

`TracksApiEndPoints` Explained

The `TracksApiEndPoints` class is a set of static data and methods so I don't instantiate it, I call the methods on the class directly e.g.

`TracksApiEndPoints.todos` gives me access to the URL for the TODOs API endpoint and I can issue `GET` or `POST` requests to that end point:

```
public static final String todos= "/todos.xml";
```

There are also methods (e.g. `todo`) which, given the `id` of a TODO in the system will return a URL that contains the `id` in the correct place so that I could `GET` (to retrieve) or `PUT` (to amend) the TODO item details. In the code the `String.format` is used to generate the partial URL String:

```java
    public static final String todoId ="/todos/%s.xml";



    public static String todo(String id) {
        return String.format(todoId, id);
    }
```

TracksApiEndPoints

Since the class is very small I list the full `class` code below:

```java
package api.version_2_3_0.tracks;

public class TracksApiEndPoints {

    public static final String todos= "/todos.xml";
    public static final String todoId ="/todos/%s.xml";
    public static final String users="/users.xml";
    public static final String projects="/projects.xml";
    public static final String projectId="/projects/%s.xml";
    public static final String contexts="/contexts.xml";
    public static final String projectIdTodos="/projects/%s/todos.xml";

    public static String project(String id) {
        return String.format(projectId, id);
    }

    public static String projectsTodos(String id) {
        return String.format(projectIdTodos, id);
    }

    public static String todo(String id) {
        return String.format(todoId, id);
    }
}
```

TracksApiEndPoints Evolution

The TracksApiEndPoints class evolved via refactoring.

Originally I had code that used String Literals e.g.

```
@Test
public void aUserCanNotAccessIfNoBasicAuthHeaderUsingGivenWhenThen(){

    given().
            contentType("text/xml").
    when().
            get("http://192.168.17.129/todos.xml").
    then().
            statusCode(401);
}
```

After creating a few tests I saw that I repeatedly used the URL `String` Literal:

- `"http://192.168.17.129/todos.xml"`

I initially refactored this into a Field constant in the test class, but then I found myself repeating it in multiple test classes.

At which point I refactored this into:

- a `TestEnv` class to represent the URL portion i.e. `http://192.168.17.129`
- a `TracksApiEndPoints` class to represent the `/todos.xml`

That way, I had one place to configure the Test Environment URL. And one place where I defined the Tracks API End points, should these ever need to change.

Once these classes existed, when I wrote test code that accessed new parts of the API, I added the new endpoints directly into `TracksApiEndPoints` since that is the class which contains all the API Endpoint information.

`TracksApiEndPoints` Coverage Review

Reviewing the `TracksApiEndPoints` gives us a pretty good idea of the coverage of the API achieved.

Any endpoint that is not mentioned in the `TracksApiEndPoints` has no coverage, so a reviewer can easily spot any high level gaps.

However, just because an endpoint is mentioned, doesn't mean that it is used. IntelliJ 'find usages' can help us identify where the endpoint is called. Ideally, the only place they are used is in the `TracksApi` class, but this might not be true given the 'example' nature of the code.

Also, just because the endpoint is used in the `TracksAPI` doesn't mean that we have covered all the verbs possible for the endpoint.

Having the URLs obvious in a single class makes it easy to start a review of the API coverage.

URLifier

I'll describe the `URLifier` here since it is a very simple class which is used by the `TestEnv` class which we will look at in more detail in the next section.

- found in `package api.version_2_3_0.tracks.http`

The `URLifier` converts a `String` to a `URL` without forcing the client code to declare that it throws a `MalformedURLException`.

```
public class URLifier {

    public static URL getURLfromString(String aString){
        try {
            return new URL(aString);
        } catch (MalformedURLException e) {
            e.printStackTrace();
            throw new RuntimeException(
                        String.format(
                        "URL %s is not correctly formatted",
                        aString));
        }
    }
}
```

I make the assumption that I know what I'm doing with this code and that I don't dynamically amend the URL.

If an error does occur during conversion then a `RuntimeException` is thrown.

Since I know the use cases of the Abstraction layer I can make decisions like this to make it easier for the client code to use the library code.

TestEnv

The TestEnv class is very simple and is used to collate all the information for a particular Tracks Test Environment.

You can find it in:

- package api.version_2_3_0.tracks

It is a wrapper for the URL of the environment, the Admin username, Admin password, and configuration of the proxy (if any) that we access the environment through.

```
public class TestEnv {

    private final String theURL;
    private final String userName;
    private final String userPassword;
    private String proxyUrl;
    private int proxyPort;
    private boolean useProxy;
```

The URL, username and password are configured via the constructor and cannot be changed once the object has been instantiated.

```
    public TestEnv(String theURL, String userName,
                                  String userPassword){
        this.theURL = theURL;
        this.userName = userName;
        this.userPassword = userPassword;
        this.useProxy = false;
    }
```

The proxy, can be configured at runtime, and we can set whether we use it at runtime or not.

```
public void configureProxy(String url, int port){
    this.proxyUrl = url;
    this.proxyPort = port;
}

public void setUseProxy(boolean useProxy) {
    this.useProxy = useProxy;
}
```

All of the other methods are accessors that return the data about the environment.

The getURL method uses the URLifier to convert a String to a URL.

```
public URL getURL() {
    return URLifier.getURLfromString(theURL);
}
```

The userProxy returns true when we have setUseProxy to true and a URL for the proxy has been configured.

```
public boolean useProxy(){
    return (useProxy && proxyUrl!=null);
}
```

The rest of the methods are simple accessors that return the data stored about the environment.

```
public String getUserName() {
    return userName;
}

public String getUserPassword() {
    return userPassword;
}

public String getProxyURL() {
    return proxyUrl;
}

public int getProxyPort() {
    return this.proxyPort;
}
```

`TracksApi`

And now the moment you've all been waiting for. The code that communicates with the API.

And... sorry, but that comes later. First I'll describe some thoughts about abstraction layers and how I implemented them.

I took the view that the API has:

- A logical level - i.e. what it does.
- A physical level - how the messages are sent and implemented.

The `TracksApi` class provides the logical level view of the Tracks API and its functionality.

The physical level is a different abstraction model and is in the `HttpMessageSender` class.

I partly take this view because I'm modelling both the usage (logical view) and the implementation (physical view) of the API calls. These are different domains, so I separate them in my code.

`TracksApi` is responsible for:

- Building the content of the messages.
- Routing messages to the correct end point.
- Selecting the correct HTTP verb to use e.g. `GET`, `PUT` etc.
- Converting the XML data returned into Domain Objects i.e. the `entity` classes.

I do not explain all of the code for the `TracksApi` here, as you can look at it in the source code:

- `src\main\java`
- `package api.version_2_3_0.tracks`
- `class TracksApi`

I will explain the common patterns so you can spot them easily when you read the source code.

`TracksApi` State

The `TracksApi` doesn't maintain much state. This is evidenced by the fields that the class has.

```
private final URL url;
private final HttpMessageSender httpMessageSender;
```

Both fields are final, so can't be changed once set.

The 'last response' is stored, and accessible through the `TracksApi` using the method `getLastResponse`, but the state is actually maintained by the `http` abstraction layer.

Creating a `TracksApi`

A `TracksApi` can be created, either by passing in a `TestEnv` or a URL, username and password.

The `TestEnv` constructor is the main one that the 'test' code uses because for most tests a single user is used.

The URL, username and password is used in the `@Test` utility to create users and setup the environment, because we create Projects and Tasks for multiple users.

```
public TracksApi(URL tracksUrl, String username,
                                 String password){
    this.url = tracksUrl;

    httpMessageSender = new HttpMessageSender(tracksUrl);
    httpMessageSender.basicAuth(username, password);
}

public TracksApi(TestEnv testEnv) {

    this(   testEnv.getURL(),
            testEnv.getUserName(),
            testEnv.getUserPassword());

    if(testEnv.useProxy()){
        proxy(testEnv.getProxyURL(), testEnv.getProxyPort());
    }
}
```

Code is shared between the two constructors. So the `TracksApi` constructor that takes a `TestEnv` uses the more explicit constructor, but since it also knows about proxies, it can configure the proxy if appropriate.

The constructor stores the url and configures the HttpMessageSender. Since Basic Auth is used for the API, the Basic Auth settings are configured during construction of the message sender.

Configuring a Proxy

```
public void proxy(String proxyURL, int proxyPort) {
    httpMessageSender.proxy(proxyURL, proxyPort);
}
```

The proxy is also controlled by the HttpMessageSender.

At the moment, the API abstraction takes the view that the client should not have to know much about the implementation of the HttpMessageSender so all configuration is done via the TracksApi.

This isolates, to some extent, the 'test' code from the 'implementation' code, although there is some bleed through with the Response object.

We can configure the proxy at any time using the public proxy method.

I often use this for debugging to see the messages sent by the @Test code and the responses received from the system.

Having the proxy easily configurable makes it possible for me to use the abstraction code for adhoc interactive testing, provided the abstraction layers support the methods I want to use.

e.g. if I want to create a Project with a specific name that is not covered by the @Test code, I can create a simple @Test method, configure the TestApi to use a proxy and then send through messages and check the response. The @Test can be very short lived and I might copy it into my exploratory test notes and delete it from the code base when finished.

Creating Entities with the TracksApi

The 'creation' methods:

- createContext to create a Context.
- createProject to create a Project.
- createTodo to create a TODO for a Project and Context.

All use the same basic format, so we will explore one, and you can view the rest in the source code.

```
public Response createContext(String aContext) {

    String tmplt = "<context><name>%s</name></context>";

    String msg = String.format(tmplt, aContext);

    Response response = httpMessageSender.postXmlMessageTo(msg,
                                    TracksApiEndPoints.contexts);

    return response;
}
```

The XML for the message is stored as a String template suitable for use in a `String.format` statement to insert the values in the message.

The XML was taken from the earlier investigation using cURL and Postman so I knew that the basic format of the message worked, before adding it into the code.

The message body `msg` is sent as a POST message by using the `HttpMessageSender` `postXmlMessageTo` method.

The endpoint URL to send the message to is taken from `TracksApiEndPoints`.

On Returning a `Response` Object

The response returned from the 'create' methods is a `RestAssured Response`, this is where the isolation between the 'Tracks' domain and the 'HTTP' domain have bled into each other.

Ideally a different `Response` object should be used - one which allows the 'HTTP' client to be completely isolated from the 'Tracks' API.

The only real uses of a `Response` object are to check the status code, parse the headers, and to parse the body text, so a simple `HttpResponse` object with these fields would have supported a better separation between the `@Test` code and the `RestAssured` library.

This split is explored more fully in a later chapter on future refactoring.

Retrieving Entities from the `TracksApi`

All the GET methods take a similar approach, so again we will just look at one of the methods in detail and you can view the rest in the source code.

In summary the GET methods:

- Call the getXMLResponseFrom method on the HttpMessageSender object, this issues a GET request, using basic authentication and with a contentType header of "text/xml".
- The body of the response is treated as a String and parsed as XML.
- The RestAssured XmlPath library is used to parse the XML.
- The String values from the XML are build up into a domain object.
- A domain object or a List of domain objects is returned from the method.

As an example we will use the getContexts method:

```java
public List<TracksContext> getContexts() {

    List<TracksContext> contexts = new ArrayList<TracksContext>();

    Response contextsListResponse=
                httpMessageSender.getXMLResponseFrom(
                                    TracksApiEndPoints.contexts);

    String xml = contextsListResponse.body().asString();

    XmlPath xmlPath = new XmlPath(xml);
    NodeChildren contextNodes =
                xmlPath.getNodeChildren(
                            "contexts.context");

    for(Node contextNode : contextNodes.list()){
        TracksContext context = new TracksContext();
        for(Node contextElement : contextNode.children().list()){
            if(contextElement.name().contentEquals("id")){
                context.setId(contextElement.value());
            }
            if(contextElement.name().contentEquals("name")){
                context.setName(contextElement.value());
            }
        }
        contexts.add(context);
    }
    return contexts;
}
```

The translation between XML and domain objects is the bulk of this method. Ideally, it should be pulled out into a new method, possibly in another class, but for the moment it is all merged in here.

The `XmlPath` class which does the XML parsing can be used independently of `RestAssured`.

- Installing XML Path Independently[121]
- XML Path Documentation[122]
- Groovy XML Manipulation[123]

We instantiate an `XmlPath` object with the contents of the message body.

```
XmlPath xmlPath = new XmlPath(xml);
```

Then we use the Groovy parsing format to extract nodes from XML.

```
NodeChildren contextNodes =
            xmlPath.getNodeChildren(
                     "contexts.context");
```

This gives us a collection of Nodes which we can iterate over and create domain objects from:

```
for(Node contextNode : contextNodes.list()){
    TracksContext context = new TracksContext();
    for(Node contextElement : contextNode.children().list()){
        if(contextElement.name().contentEquals("id")){
            context.setId(contextElement.value());
        }
        if(contextElement.name().contentEquals("name")){
            context.setName(contextElement.value());
        }
    }
    contexts.add(context);
}
```

Amending Tracks Entities

We amend entities in Tracks by using a PUT HTTP message.

The PUT messages are implemented by the `HttpMessageSender` class.

In the example code we have one amendment method, to amend a Project.

---

[121] https://github.com/rest-assured/rest-assured/wiki/GettingStarted#xmlpath
[122] http://static.javadoc.io/io.rest-assured/xml-path/3.0.1/io/restassured/path/xml/XmlPath.html
[123] http://www.groovy-lang.org/processing-xml.html#_manipulating_xml

```java
public Response amendProject(String projectId,
                             Map<String, String> fieldsToAmend) {

    StringBuilder messageBody = new StringBuilder();

    messageBody.append("<project>");

    for(String key: fieldsToAmend.keySet()){
        messageBody.append(String.format("<%s>", key));
        String value = fieldsToAmend.get(key);
        if(value!=null){
            messageBody.append(value);
        }
        messageBody.append(String.format("</%s>", key));
    }

    messageBody.append("</project>");

    return httpMessageSender.putXmlMessageTo(
                        TracksApiEndPoints.project(projectId),
                        messageBody.toString());
}
```

The amendment class takes a `Map` of fields which are iterated over to create an XML body for the message.

Deleting Entities

Deleting an entity simply requires using the `HttpMessageSender` class to issue a `DELETE` call on an endpoint.

```java
public Response deleteProject(String projectId) {
    return httpMessageSender.deleteMessage(
                    TracksApiEndPoints.project(projectId));
}
```

Domain Objects

The domain objects are all very simple classes which store and retrieve values.

- src\main\java
- package api.version_2_3_0.tracks.entity

e.g. the TracksContext is just a simple Java object

```java
public class TracksContext {
    private String id;
    private String name;

    public void setId(String value) {
        this.id = value;
    }

    public void setName(String value) {
        this.name = value;
    }

    public String id() {
        return this.id;
    }
}
```

Summary

The TracksApi methods offer a 'logical' view of the Tracks API.

They could be more separate from the physical implementation if, instead of returning a RestAssured Response object, they returned a TracksResponse object.

The aim of a TracksApi abstraction layer is to make sure that the person using the API does not have to know the innards of how the API works.

Supporting a proxy is very important to allow abstraction code to support both automated @Test execution and adhoc interactive execution.

The message code in the TracksApi was taken from the experiments conducted with cURL and Postman so we were fairly confident that they would work. Also if something goes wrong when sending a message, we can use HTTP Debug Proxies, Postman and cURL to help debug the abstraction layers.

The Case Study - Sending HTTP Calls using REST Assured

As you have seen throughout the preceding chapters, REST Assured is not used everywhere within the project.

This is not because RestAssured is 'bad' - on the contrary, I use it as my default REST library because it is so easy to use.

The reason it isn't more used is because most of the time I don't want to write code that is written at the HTTP or physical REST level.

Most of the time, I want to use abstraction layers that make it easy for me to send messages, and then I want to assert on the responses in a way that is appropriate for the @Test code.

I also want to support interactive investigation.

Let's now have a look at the actual HttpMessageSender that has most of the RestAssured dependencies.

This will also allow us to discuss some of the nuances of RestAssured.

HttpMessageSender

The HttpMessageSender class has a single constructor, and it basically sets the protocol, domain name and top level path.

```
public HttpMessageSender(URL aUrl) {
    this.url = aUrl;
}
```

This means that from now on we can call methods and only pass in the final elements of the path and any query parameter and fragment.

- protocol://domain:port/path/query#fragment

Proxy Control

The proxy method is public and can be called on an HttpMessageSender object at any time.

```
public void proxy(String proxyURL, int proxyPort) {
    if(proxyURL!=null) {
        RestAssured.proxy(proxyURL, proxyPort);
    }
}
```

From the above you can see that, assuming a `proxyURL` is supplied, we call the `proxy` method on `RestAssured` to set the proxy.

A few things to note, because most `RestAssured` calls are made statically:

- It is the same `RestAssured` instance making the calls.
- Each `RestAssured` call requires passing in all the parameters e.g. session ids, cookies, headers etc.
- Once the `RestAssured` proxy is configured for one call, it is configured for all future calls.

Another way to control the proxy, rather than call the `RestAssured.proxy` method, is to use the Java virtual machine proxy configuration.

```
-Dhttp.proxyHost=localhost -Dhttp.proxyPort=8080
```

These can be set in the run configuration in the IDE or on the command line when running your code.

- docs.oracle.com/javase/8/docs/technotes/guides/net/proxies.html[124]

Basic Auth

The Tracks API requires Basic Auth to be used, with the username and parameter encoded as a basic authentication header on the message.

A Basic Auth header has the header name `Authorization` with the value `"Basic dXN1-cjpiaXRuYW1p"`. Where the string `dXN1cjpiaXRuYW1p` is a base64 encoded representation of "username:password".

If you decode[125] `dXN1cjpiaXRuYW1p` then you'll see the text is a 'base64' encoded version of `"user:bitnami"`

In the `HttpMessageSender` we have a `basicAuth` method which uses the same username and password for each message after they are set.

---

[124] http://docs.oracle.com/javase/8/docs/technotes/guides/net/proxies.html
[125] https://www.base64decode.org

```
public void basicAuth(String user, String password) {
    this.authUser = user;
    this.authPassword = password;
}
```

There are no guards or protections against a user of the API abstraction code not setting the authentication username and password. This code was not written to be robust for use by other programmers.

These variables are used when sending a message e.g.

```
given().
    auth().preemptive().basic(authUser, authPassword).
```

If I use `auth` without `preemtive` mode then RestAssured initially sends a request without authentication headers to the server to see what authentication the server asks for, before sending a request with the authentication header e.g.

- `.auth().basic(authUser, authPassword).`

This effectively sends two messages, one without an `Authorization` header, immediately followed by one with the `Authorization` header.

I could add the authorisation header myself, so that only one message is sent, but if the authentication scheme changes then I have to handle it, and I have to encode the username/password myself. e.g.

- `header(new Header("Authorization", "Basic dXNlcjpiaXRuYW1p")).`

When I use 'pre-emptive' mode (as illustrated by the code excerpt below) rather than 'challenge' mode, then only a single HTTP message is sent and RestAssured creates and adds the `Authorization` header for us with the username and password i.e.

- `auth().preemptive().basic(authUser, authPassword).`

Post a Form

You have already seen this code when we discussed the "App as API".

```
public Response postFormMessageTo(String msg, String endpoint){
    return postFormMessageTo(msg, endpoint, anEmptyCookieJar());
}

public Response postFormMessageTo(String msg, String endpoint,
                                  Map<String, String> cookieJar){
    return postMessageTo(msg, endpoint,
            "application/x-www-form-urlencoded", cookieJar);
}
```

Because we are using `HttpMessageSender` as our HTTP abstraction, we can also use it to send messages to the server which look like form submissions.

A form submission has the content type header set to the value `"application/x-www-form-urlencoded"`.

Post an XML Message

The `TracksApi` 'create' methods don't send form messages, they send XML messages.

```
public Response postXmlMessageTo(String msg, String endpoint){
    return postMessageTo(msg, endpoint,
                    "text/xml", anEmptyCookieJar());
}
```

The XML messages have the content type header set to the value `"text/xml"`. We don't send any cookies since they use Basic Auth, rather than cookies, for authentication.

This is made obvious in the code by the use of a private method called `anEmptyCookieJar` which simply returns an empty `Map`.

```
private HashMap<String,String> anEmptyCookieJar(){
    return new HashMap<String,String>();
}
```

Use REST Assured to POST HTTP Message

I use `RestAssured` syntax to send a `POST` message to the server:

```
private Response postMessageTo(String msg, String endpoint,
                              String contentType,
                              Map<String, String> cookieJar){

    URL theEndPointUrl = createEndPointURL(url, endpoint);

    Response ret =
            given().
                    auth().preemptive().
                        basic(authUser, authPassword).
                    body(msg).
                    contentType(contentType).
                    cookies(cookieJar).
            when().
                    post(theEndPointUrl.toExternalForm()).
            andReturn();

    // ignore CREATED UNAUTHORIZED CONFLICT
    if( ret.statusCode()!=201 && ret.statusCode()!=401 &&
        ret.statusCode()!=409 ){
        System.out.println("POTENTIAL BUG - " +
                        ret.statusCode() + " FOR " +
                        endpoint + "\n" + msg );
    }

    return setLastResponse(ret);
}
```

The above code uses a private method createEndPointURL which serves the same purpose as the URLifier class that you saw earlier. It converts a String to a URL without forcing the programmer to handle a MalformedURLException.

To enable use of RestAssured the import for given, is performed statically.

```
import static io.restassured.RestAssured.given;
```

The following code shows the usage of RestAssured to actually issue a POST message:

```
Response ret =
        given().
                auth().preemptive().
                    basic(authUser, authPassword).
                body(msg).
                contentType(contentType).
                cookies(cookieJar).
        when().
                post(theEndPointUrl.toExternalForm()).
        andReturn();
```

The above code uses the `given when` syntax from `RestAssured`.

All of our 'setup' is contained in the `given` block.

- Given
    - pre-emptive Basic Auth for `authUser` with `authPassword`
        * `auth().preemptive().basic(authUser, authPassword).`
    - and a body of the HTTP message being the `msg` string
        * `body(msg).`
    - and the "contentType" header of the message set to variable `contentType`
        * `contentType(contentType).`
    - and using the cookies from the supplied `Map` variable `cookieJar`
        * `cookies(cookieJar).`
- When
    - we issue a `POST` message to URL `theEndPointUrl`
        * `post(theEndPointUrl.toExternalForm()).`
    - return the `Response` object so we can process it.
        * `andReturn();`

The method also contains some helpful utility code to report any potential issues to the console:

```
    // ignore CREATED UNAUTHORIZED CONFLICT
    if( ret.statusCode()!=201 && ret.statusCode()!=401 &&
        ret.statusCode()!=409 ){
        System.out.println("POTENTIAL BUG - " +
                            ret.statusCode() + " FOR " +
                            endpoint + "\n" + msg );
    }
```

The above code assumes that the following status codes are 'normal' for a POST message, but the user should be notified of any other status codes:

- 201 - Created
- 401 - Unauthorized
- 409 - Conflict

Anything other than these status codes will result in a "Potential Bug" message being printed out to the System console. The automated execution is not interrupted because these messages are to support human review, not automated execution.

Finally, the Response is stored to allow later code to retrieve it for asserting against if necessary:

```
    return setLastResponse(ret);
```

The setLastResponse method is a private method which stores the response and then returns it.

```
    private Response setLastResponse(Response ret) {
        lastResponse = ret;
        return ret;
    }
```

HTTP Verbs

POST is used to 'create' entities in the system.

This is implemented by the RestAssured construct:

```
post(theEndPointUrl.toExternalForm()).
```

You can expect to see similar patterns for the other `RestAssured` verb implementations:

- `GET` - to retrieve information from the system

```
get(theEndPointUrl.toExternalForm()).
```

- `PUT` - to amend an entity

```
put(theEndPointUrl.toExternalForm()).
```

- `DELETE` - to delete an entity

```
delete(theEndPointUrl.toExternalForm()).
```

You will now see each of the above patterns in the context of their associated `HttpMessage-Sender` method.

`GET` HTTP Method Implemented with REST Assured

`GET` follows much the same pattern as the `POST` message:

- `GET` messages use a `"text/xml"` content type because every Tracks API `GET` call returns an XML payload.

```
public Response getXMLResponseFrom(String endpoint) {

    URL theEndPointUrl = createEndPointURL(url, endpoint);

    Response ret =
            given().
                    auth().preemptive().
                            basic(authUser, authPassword).
                    contentType("text/xml").
            get(theEndPointUrl.toExternalForm()).
            andReturn();

    return setLastResponse(ret);
}
```

The code also contains a getResponseFrom method which has a more generic content type header, but that is only used in the "App as API":

```
String ct = "text/html,application/xhtml+xml," +
            "application/xml;q=0.9,*/*;q=0.8";
```

PUT **HTTP Method Implemented with REST Assured**

PUT follows the same pattern as the POST message:

- Two methods, one with an empty cookie jar and one which uses a given cookie jar.
- PUT messages use a "text/xml" content type because every Tracks API GET call returns and expects an XML payload.
- The only form of the PUT method actually called by the TracksApi is the one without a cookie jar.

```java
public Response putXmlMessageTo(String endpoint, String msg) {
    return putXmlMessageTo(endpoint, msg, anEmptyCookieJar());
}

public Response putXmlMessageTo(String endpoint, String msg,
                               Map<String, String> cookieJar) {

    URL theEndPointUrl = createEndPointURL(url, endpoint);

    Response ret =
            given().
                    auth().preemptive().
                            basic(authUser, authPassword).
                    body(msg).contentType("text/xml").
                    cookies(cookieJar).
            when().
                    put(theEndPointUrl.toExternalForm()).
            andReturn();

    return setLastResponse(ret);
}
```

DELETE HTTP Method Implemented with REST Assured

DELETE also follows the same pattern as the POST message:

- Two methods, one with an empty cookie jar and one which uses a given cookie jar.
- DELETE messages use a normal generic content type because we don't expect to receive any information in the body of the response, the status code should tell us if the entity was deleted or not.
- The only form of the DELETE method actually called by the TracksApi is the one without a cookie jar.

```
public Response deleteMessage(String endpoint){
    return deleteMessage(endpoint, anEmptyCookieJar() );
}

public Response deleteMessage(String endpoint,
                             Map<String, String> cookieJar) {
    URL theEndPointUrl = createEndPointURL(url, endpoint);

    String ct= "text/html,application/xhtml+xml,"+
               "application/xml;q=0.9,*/*;q=0.8";

    Response ret =
            given().
                auth().preemptive().
                            basic(authUser, authPassword).
                cookies(cookieJar).
                contentType(ct).
              delete(theEndPointUrl.toExternalForm()).
              andReturn();

    return setLastResponse(ret);
}
```

Summary

Only a very small portion of REST Assured functionality is actually used. This is because I created a set of code that models a higher level of abstraction to interact with the `TracksApi`.

This is due to the type of testing conducted. The testing was very high level and basically:

- Can I create a Project?
- Can I amend a Project?
- etc.

If I was testing at a lower level e.g.

- When I send a `POST` request to the Project end point with a `text/html` header, does the system reject it?

Then I would probably use the `RestAssured` library in more detail because I would need more frequent access to the HTTP features.

I might still decide to create a higher level abstraction layer to make the test code readable and maintainable, but it would need to support more complex message configuration.

I probably still wouldn't use the REST Assured assertions since I prefer to use either a separate Assertion library or the Assertion library built into the Test Runner - in this case JUnit.

The Case Study - the `Test` Code Explored

Now on to the 'Test' code.

The 'test' code is all in the folder hierarchy:

- `src\test\java`

The above folder contains a mix of:

- Unit tests for the Random Test Data Generation - which is described in a later chapter.
- Unit tests for some of the abstraction layers.
- Support class for Test Environment configuration `TestEnvDefaults`.
- Utility `@Test` methods for data creation which was covered in an earlier chapter.
- Support classes for synchronisation.
- `@Test` methods to check for functional conditions in the execution of the REST API.

What Makes It 'test'?

What helps the programmer decide if a class is added to the 'test' folder hierarchy, as opposed to the 'main' folder?

If the project is purely aimed at automating, and primarily for testing i.e. there is no production application code, then:

- Use 'main' for abstractions.
- Use 'test' for adhoc utility `@Test` methods, unit tests and `@Test` methods that would be run automatically e.g. during CI.

The above are guidelines, rather than absolute rules as different projects will make different decisions. But these are the guidelines I default to.

The code in 'main' is the library code used in @Test methods, but could also be packaged as a .jar to support other projects to automate the application.

Looking at the code in 'test', you will see that most of it fits into this description.

There are a few classes that don't:

- TracksResponseProcessor given a response will extract an id from a header. This could validly be moved to 'main'.
- Wait in the synchronisation package could also be moved to the 'main' folder.

The above could justifiably be moved to the 'main' since they might be of use to other projects.

They represent a form of Technical Debt, simply because of the way the code has been written.

TestEnvDefaults

TestEnvDefaults is a configuration class to make it easy to create a TestEnv object that represents the test environment. This is only used for the 'test' methods so I added it to the 'test' folder. Any other code that wants to use TestEnv can instantiate a TestEnv of its own, and this is in the 'main' folder.

You saw snippets of TestEnvDefaults when we were looking at the test data creation utility test.

You can find it in the source code:

- src\test\java
- package api.version_2_3_0.environmentconfig

It is a simple class used as a central place to configure the test environment location.

```java
public class TestEnvDefaults {
    public static final String theURL = "http://192.168.126.129";
    public static final String adminUserName="user";
    public static final String adminUserPassword="bitnami";
    public static final String proxyUrl="localhost";
    public static final int proxyPort=8000;

    public static URL getURL() {
        return URLifier.getURLfromString(theURL);
    }

    public static String getAdminUserName() {
        return adminUserName;
    }

    public static String getAdminUserPassword() {
        return adminUserPassword;
    }

    public static String getProxyUrl() {
        return proxyUrl;
    }

    public static int getProxyPort() {
        return proxyPort;
    }

    public static TestEnv getTestEnv(){
        TestEnv env = new TestEnv(theURL, adminUserName, adminUserPassword);
        env.configureProxy(proxyUrl, proxyPort);
        env.setUseProxy(false);
        return env;
    }
}
```

The above class works well for the code given its current use case scenarios.

Currently:

- The code is used to support exercises and workshops.
- The tests are run from the IDE.

- The environments are not stable, they are VMs run on individual machines and change frequently.
- Tests are run for the purpose of learning how to automate a REST API rather than validate the function of the API so forcing people to amend the code helps them learn the code.

If the tests were run from CI on a regular basis then the above would not be good enough.

We might have defaults in a class to support local execution, but we would want the ability to override them during a CI process to point the tests at a specific environment.

This would likely be done by having the `static` fields:

- Not be `final` - so they can be changed by the code.
- Not be `public` - so they are only changed by code in the class.
- Use lazy instantiation,
    - so that they default to `null`,
    - when they are accessed then we would check if they were set to `null`, and if so we would check for environment variables or system properties which can override hard coded defaults.
    - if no environment or system properties exist then set the values to hard coded defaults - coded as constants in the class.

In some production environments, the use of hard coded defaults would be viewed as dangerous because they might slip into production. As a result, we might choose not to have the `TestEnvDefaults` as a static class and instead force it to be instantiated. We might also have the values configured externally to the code using:

- environment variables,
- system properties,
- property file,
- etc.

Currently this code works well as an example, but this may not be a pattern that you want to use in your production test code.

Synchronisation

Synchronisation is an incredibly important concept for robust automated execution.

Synchronisation means that we wait for the application to be in a particular state before we interact with it i.e. we synchronise with it to make sure it is ready.

If we get 'out of sync' with the application and try to exercise functionality before the application is ready to receive input then we can receive errors and the automated execution can fail.

Very often it can be hard to identify the reason for failures, and people often say that they have 'random' test failures or 'flaky' tests.

The root cause of much 'flakiness' in automated execution can often relate to ineffective synchronisation.

REST APIs have an inbuilt and very effective synchronisation mechanism since the synchronisation is inherent in the message passing process.

- We send a message to the API.
- We wait until we receive a response.

Sometimes we have to have extra synchronisation for polling:

- The API might be supporting a polling mechanism where we initiate a long running task with an API call and then poll to check for completion.
- We might build synchronisation code that offers us a 'wait' by polling the API until the results are ready.

We may have to add additional synchronisation layers for particular application functionality or processing.

Synchronisation with `Wait`

The `Wait` class is in:

- src\test\java

- package api.version_2_3_0.synchronisation

This wait class is a 'time based wait'. i.e. wait for 2 seconds

Very often people have an immediate reaction to a 'time based wait'.

"Time Based Waits Are Bad"

I share this reaction.

I think it is a bad idea to wait for a certain period of time if you are trying to wait for application state.

e.g. in the previous example of a polling mechanism. If, we tried to synchronise on the polling mechanism with a 'time based wait' then a naive synchronisation would look as follows:

- Issue a request.
- Wait 5 seconds for results to be available.
- Call API to get results.
- Carry on regardless and fail if no results received.

Sometimes the above process would work, but sometimes it might take longer than 5 seconds for the results to be available, in which case the synchronisation would 'randomly' fail.

A polling synchronisation would be more like:

- Issue a request.
- While we have not received results,
    – wait one second,
    – call API to get results,
    – if 15 seconds have passed then break out of this loop with a Timeout Error.

While the above has a time component, since it calls the API every 1 second and "times out" after 15 seconds, it is really synchronising on the results. It is just using the timing to avoid flooding the API with calls, and avoid an infinite loop.

The Timeout is set to the MAXIMUM that we would ever want to wait, and if it took longer than this we would consider it an error.

Time Based Waits Are Bad Unless...

Time Based waits are bad unless you are actually trying to synchronise on a period of time.

In the case of the Wait method in the code, we are waiting for the passage of time.

```java
public class Wait {
    public static void aFewSeconds(int seconds) {
        try {
            Thread.sleep(seconds * 1000);
        } catch (InterruptedException e) {
            e.printStackTrace();
        }
    }
}
```

This makes more sense in the context of the test that uses it:

```java
        api.createProject(newProjectName);
        Assert.assertEquals(201, api.getLastResponse().
                                            getStatusCode());



        Wait.aFewSeconds(2);
        // so that when we compare update times they are different



        TracksProject amendedProject = api.getProject(projectId);
        // check amended date has changed
        Assert.assertFalse(amendedProject.getUpdatedAt().
                        contentEquals(
                                createdProject.getUpdatedAt()));
        // check created is the same
        Assert.assertTrue(amendedProject.getCreatedAt().
                        contentEquals(
                                createdProject.getCreatedAt()));
```

In the above code we:

- Create a Project.

- Wait 2 seconds.
- Amend a Project.
- Compare the created date with the amended date to ensure the amended date has updated.

If we didn't wait for time to pass then the amended date might not change on the record (depending on the granularity of the time recording on the records) e.g. if the time is reported in seconds, and an amendment is made within a few milliseconds then the same date/time value can be in created date and amended date, even after amending, because we didn't roll into a new second of time.

In this situation a "time based wait" is a valid approach

Also, this no longer looks like Technical Debt, it looks like premature optimisation.

This 'wait' is only performed in one test. It should probably be a private method in the actual @Test class or an inner class within the @Test class. Then if we have to use a time based wait in another test, it would be useful to move it out into a class of its own to reuse the code.

TracksResponseProcessor

The TracksResponseProcessor is a very simple class which processes a Response from one of the REST API calls and extracts some information.

```java
public class TracksResponseProcessor {
    private final Response response;

    public TracksResponseProcessor(Response response) {
        this.response = response;
    }

    public String getIdFromLocation() {
        String location = response.getHeader("location");
        String[] urlChunks = location.split("/");
        String id = urlChunks[urlChunks.length-1];
        return id;
    }
}
```

Very often when making calls to REST APIs the headers are used to report information back. In the use case for this method:

- Create a Project in Tracks.
- A 201 status is received with no content.
- The location header in the response is used to tell you where you can find the new Project.

The location header has the id embedded in the URL so we parse the value in the location header.

The REST Assured getHeader method is used to get the URL value of the location header. Then perform a crude split on the URL and take the last item from the array.

e.g.

- Given a URL like "http://localhost/projects/12".
- A split by "/" would create an array of length 4, containing:
    - [0] "http:",
    - [1] localhost,
    - [2] projects,
    - [3] 12.
- Find the last item in the array (4-1) = [3].
- The last item in the array is the id we want.

For a more complicated URL we would probably use the Regular Expression classes from Java.

e.g.

- Given a URL like "http://localhost/projects/12.xml"
- a regular expression like [\S]+?\/projects\/(\d+)\.xml would capture the digits "12" in the (\d+)

In Java we would perform this type of extract as follows:

```
String findLocation = "[\\S]+?/projects/(\\d+)\\.xml";

Pattern p = Pattern.compile(findLocation);

Matcher m = p.matcher(location);

String projectId = "";
if (m.find()) {
    projectId = m.group(1);
}
```

projectId would contain the digits "12".

Summary

This chapter has provided an overview of the 'test' folder and tried to explain the contents of this folder and the reasons why some classes are in the 'test' folder and not in the 'main' folder.

It also described the main support classes for 'test' code.

The next chapter will look at the actual @Test methods that use the support classes and the abstraction layers.

The Case Study - the Authentication @Test Methods Explored

Now, the moment you have been waiting for, the actual @Test methods themselves.

The tests were written in a certain order:

- Authentication
- Project
- Tasks and Actions

Hopefully the ordering makes sense.

Authentication tests come first because if we can't automate authentication then we can't move on to automate other parts of the API. The ability to automate Authentication is a pre-requisite for automating other parts of the API.

Projects follow, because they are one of the top level entities and you can't create Tasks without Projects.

Tackle Tasks after everything else because we will then have the basic entities, abstractions and code in place to automate them.

Evolving the Authentication Tests

The main authentication tests are in:

- src\test\java
- AuthenticationTest

When you look at the code you will see a mix of tests that use RestAssured, HttpMessage-Sender and they do not use the TracksApi. I will explain the reasons for that.

The authentication tests demonstrate the evolution of the test code.

Initially, all the @Test methods in AuthenticationTest looked like the @Test methods in RestAssuredAuthenticationExamplesTest.

I started with a simple @Test method that used REST Assured directly, with hard coded values:

- environment IP
- endpoint URL
- username and password

e.g.

```
@Test
public void aUserCanAccessWithBasicAuthHeaderUsingRestAssured(){

    given().
            contentType("text/xml").
            auth().preemptive().basic("user", "bitnami").
    expect().
            statusCode(200).
    when().
            get("http://192.168.17.129/todos.xml");
}
```

This was then refactored to create the TestEnvDefaults class and TracksApiEndPoints class:

```
@Test
public void aUserCanAccessWithBasicAuthHeader(){

    given().
            contentType("text/xml").
            auth().preemptive().basic(
                    TestEnvDefaults.getAdminUserName(),
                    TestEnvDefaults.getAdminUserPassword()).
    expect().
            statusCode(200).
    when().
            get(TestEnvDefaults.getURL().toExternalForm() +
                TracksApiEndPoints.todos);
}
```

Then further refactored to create the HttpMessageSender class:

```
@Test
public void aUserCanAuthenticateAndUseAPIWithBasicAuth(){

    HttpMessageSender http = new HttpMessageSender(
                                    TestEnvDefaults.getURL());
    // setup the sender to use a proxy
    //http.proxy(TestEnvDefaults.getProxyUrl(),
    //          TestEnvDefaults.getProxyPort());

    http.basicAuth( TestEnvDefaults.getAdminUserName(),
                TestEnvDefaults.getAdminUserPassword());

    Response response = http.getResponseFrom(
                            TracksApiEndPoints.todos);

    Assert.assertEquals(200, response.getStatusCode());
}
```

You can see from comments in the above code that I was also experimenting with the proxy configuration.

Instead of using REST Assured assertions in the @Test method, I used JUnit assertions.

AuthenticationTest

Although the AuthenticationTest class has multiple @Test methods - this is purely for the sake of documenting the example.

The AuthenticationTest methods do not use the TracksApi because they are working at a more basic level.

These tests operate at the HTTP level. They basically check that the correct response is received when an HTTP request is sent with authentication.

Although I would prefer most of the test code to use the HttpMessageSender I would still keep the REST Assured based test aUserCanNotAccessIfNoBasicAuthHeader here.

```
@Test
public void aUserCanNotAccessIfNoBasicAuthHeader(){

    given().
            contentType("text/html,application/xhtml+xml," +
                        "application/xml;q=0.9,*/*;q=0.8").
    expect().
            statusCode(401).
    when().
            get(TestEnvDefaults.getURL().toExternalForm() +
                    TracksApiEndPoints.todos);
}
```

This is because abstraction layers 'hide' functionality from you as a user of that Abstraction.

- HttpMessageSender is designed to enforce use of a Basic Auth header.
  - We can use HttpMessageSender to test for valid passwords, and invalid username password combinations, but not for testing a message sent without a Basic Auth header.
  - The class is designed to make it easy to send HTTP messages to Tracks.
- REST Assured has no such constraints, it allows the sending of messages without HTTP authentication.

For most of our tests we don't want to be forced to remember to add the Basic Auth header, we leave that job up to the Abstraction Layer (HttpMessageSender).

It is still important to test what happens if no Auth header is present at all. To test that, we drop down to the actual HTTP abstraction. Our HTTP abstraction is REST Assured.

We could just as easily use HttpClient or one of the other HTTP libraries for this.

I could rewrite HttpMessageSender to support sending a message without a Basic Auth header, but since I only really need to test that absence in one or two tests, it didn't make sense to clutter HttpMessageSender with the added complexity that this flexibility would require.

As a result, if I did decide to move away from REST Assured, I would also have to rewrite the tests which rely on the raw HTTP abstraction that REST Assured provides.

Final Test

The final test in the `AuthenticationTest` class is an `@Test` method to check that a user can not access the API with a username and password that do not exist in the system.

```
@Test
public void aUserCanNotAccessIfNotAuthenticatedWithBasicAuth(){

    RandomDataGenerator wordGenerator = new RandomDataGenerator();

    HttpMessageSender http = new HttpMessageSender(
                                    TestEnvDefaults.getURL());

    // add basic auth but with wrong details
    http.basicAuth( TestEnvDefaults.getAdminUserName()
                            + wordGenerator.randomWord(),
                    TestEnvDefaults.getAdminUserPassword()
                            + wordGenerator.randomWord());

    Response response = http.getResponseFrom(
                                    TracksApiEndPoints.todos);
    Assert.assertEquals(401, response.getStatusCode());
}
```

This creates a set of invalid user authentication details by adding a random word to the username and to the password.

The random word is generated using a very simple approach:

```
public class RandomDataGenerator {
    public String randomWord() {
        return String.valueOf(System.currentTimeMillis()).
                replaceAll("1", "a").
                replaceAll("2", "d").
                replaceAll("3", "o").
                replaceAll("4", "n").
                replaceAll("5", "e").
                replaceAll("6", "r").
                replaceAll("7", "t").
                replaceAll("8", "h").
                replaceAll("9", "i").
```

```
                        replaceAll("0", "s");
    }
}
```

The above code creates a `String` from the current time in milliseconds and then replaces each digit with a letter e.g. 1234567890 would become `adonerthis`.

I made the decision to add this `RandomDataGenerator` into the `src\main\java` folder hierarchy because of its re-use potential.

You can find it in the package:

- package `api.version_2_3_0.testdata`

Summary

The `AuthenticationTest` is the lowest level type of test examples in this code base.

There are times when we need to test REST APIs at a very low HTTP level and the raw HTTP Client libraries are a good choice for this type of testing.

Abstraction layers 'hide' information and can make it difficult to test certain types of functionality.

We face a choice of expanding abstraction layers to cope with these extra conditions or, accepting that we need to use multiple levels of abstraction and use layers that support combination to achieve the coverage that we want.

The Case Study - the Project @Test Methods Explored

The Project @Test methods in the class ProjectTest demonstrate the level of testing that takes advantage of the TracksApi abstractions.

These @Test methods do not use RestAssured and HttpMessageSender directly because they are exploring entity level API messages, rather than HTTP format and endpoint access.

The ProjectTest class only covers three basic scenarios, but this was enough to flush out TracksApi abstraction to cover GET, POST, PUT and DELETE scenarios.

Create Project

All of the REST API interaction in this test is carried out through the TracksApi abstraction.

Points to note:

- The simple random data generator RandomDataGenerator is used to create unique test data into the environment.
- Assertions use the JUnit assertions rather than REST Assured.
- RestAssured is used, but only because of a bleed over of the Response class.
- I named the instantiated TracksApi variable as api. This results in the test being easy to read and understand because it is not cluttered by the actual implementation details of the API calls.

```
@Test
public void aUserCanCreateAProject(){

    TracksApi api = new TracksApi(TestEnvDefaults.getTestEnv());

    // get the current set of projects
    int totalProjectsForUser = api.getProjects().size();

    // create a new project
    String newProjectName = "A New Project" +
                            new RandomDataGenerator().randomWord();
    Response response = api.createProject(newProjectName);
    Assert.assertEquals(201, response.getStatusCode());

    // get projects again and check the new project is in the list
    List<TracksProject> theProjects = api.getProjects();
    int newTotalProjectsForUser = theProjects.size();
    Assert.assertTrue(newTotalProjectsForUser >
                      totalProjectsForUser);

    Boolean foundProject = false;
    for(TracksProject project : theProjects){
        if(project.getName().contentEquals(newProjectName)){
            foundProject = true;
        }
    }
    Assert.assertTrue("Could not find project named " +
                      newProjectName, foundProject);
}
```

A few words about the assertions.

- After creating a Project through the API and asserting on the response status code.

```
Response response = api.createProject(newProjectName);
Assert.assertEquals(201, response.getStatusCode());
```

- Check that the size of the Project list has increased.

```
List<TracksProject> theProjects = api.getProjects();
int newTotalProjectsForUser = theProjects.size();
Assert.assertTrue(newTotalProjectsForUser >
                        totalProjectsForUser);
```

- Also check that the Project created was actually returned in the list of Projects.

```
Boolean foundProject = false;
for(TracksProject project : theProjects){
    if(project.getName().contentEquals(newProjectName)){
        foundProject = true;
    }
}
Assert.assertTrue("Could not find project named " +
                    newProjectName, foundProject);
```

This might be viewed as overkill, but it avoids false positives where the total has increased, but the created value is not accessible.

- The size check is performed first, because if the list hasn't increased in size then we wouldn't expect to find the Project, and there is no point spending time working through the list.

Amend

The 'amend' test creates a Project, and even repeats some of the assertions from the 'Create' test. i.e. checking for a 201 status code on creation.

Some people would view this as duplication and would not have the assertion for status code in this test. But I have retained it because if something goes wrong in the Amend assertions I want to make sure that the Project was actually created before I try to amend it.

I don't want to re-use data from the Create test, and nor do I want to make tests dependent upon each other.

Also the abstraction layer means that repeating these assertions does not take up much code and doesn't add to the maintenance overhead of the test.

This is the test that uses the 'time based wait" synchronisation.

```
@Test
public void aUserCanAmendAProjectName(){

    TracksApi api = new TracksApi(TestEnvDefaults.getTestEnv());

    // create a new project
    String newProjectName =
                    "A New Project" +
                    new RandomDataGenerator().randomWord();

    api.createProject(newProjectName);
    Assert.assertEquals(201, api.getLastResponse().
                                        getStatusCode());

    String projectId = new TracksResponseProcessor(
                            api.getLastResponse())
                                .getIdFromLocation();
    TracksProject createdProject = api.getProject(projectId);
    Assert.assertEquals(newProjectName, createdProject.getName());

    Wait.aFewSeconds(2);
    // so that when we compare update times they are different

    // amend the project

    Map<String,String> fieldsToAmend =
                                new HashMap<String,String>();
    fieldsToAmend.put("name", "the new name " +
                    new RandomDataGenerator().randomWord());

    api.amendProject(projectId, fieldsToAmend );

    TracksProject amendedProject = api.getProject(projectId);
    // check amended date has changed
    Assert.assertFalse(amendedProject.getUpdatedAt().
                    contentEquals(
                            createdProject.getUpdatedAt()));
    // check created is the same
    Assert.assertTrue(amendedProject.getCreatedAt().
                    contentEquals(
                            createdProject.getCreatedAt()));

    // check name changed
```

```
Assert.assertEquals(fieldsToAmend.get("name"),
                        amendedProject.getName());

}
```

Delete

Given the extremes that I went to in the Create test to make sure that the Project was in the list after being created. It seems that I was a little more lax with the Delete test since I only check that the system reports the Project as missing with a 404 rather than getting the full list of Projects and checking through the list.

```
@Test
public void aUserCanDeleteAProject(){

    TracksApi api = new TracksApi(TestEnvDefaults.getTestEnv());

    api.createProject("A New Project" +
                        new RandomDataGenerator().randomWord());
    Assert.assertEquals(201,
                        api.getLastResponse().getStatusCode());
    String projectId = new TracksResponseProcessor(
                                api.getLastResponse())
                                    .getIdFromLocation();

    // check we can get it
    api.getProject(projectId);
    Assert.assertEquals(200,
                        api.getLastResponse().getStatusCode());

    // check we can delete it
    api.deleteProject(projectId);
    Assert.assertEquals(200,
                        api.getLastResponse().getStatusCode());

    // check it has been deleted
    api.getProject(projectId);
    Assert.assertEquals(404,
                        api.getLastResponse().getStatusCode());
}
```

I suspect that if I encountered a bug in the system with deletes then I might expand the test to GET all the Projects and iterate through the list.

I would do this by extracting the foundProject loop in the Create test (via an extract to method refactor) to an isProjectInList method in this class and then using it in this test.

At the moment this test only covers the basic conditions.

Summary

These tests provide a useful opportunity for discussing how much we should assert, and how much we should test.

In theory, I could have combined the Create and the Amend test, since I have to create a Project before I can amend it. I could even have created, amended and then deleted in the same test and had a single test in this class.

One of the many guidelines around creating @Test methods is that "the @Test should only have one assert". Clearly I don't do that. I think it is appropriate to assert on whatever you need to.

My guiding rule was more like "the @Test should only have one intent". So I have a 'Create' test, an 'Amend' test and a 'Delete' test. I don't control the order that tests run in, so in theory, if a 'create' failed then all the tests would fail. But because I have a 'Create' test, I know that if it fails, then I would investigate that failure first.

The 'Create' and 'Amend' both have fairly weak coverage. After identifying that a 'Create' works, I would normally have some data driven tests for covering more of the create conditions e.g. different lengths of name, different characters in names, can't create with no name, etc.

Similarly the 'Amend' test is crying out for more coverage.

But, these tests are to demonstrate mechanisms, rather than serve as good examples of effective condition coverage.

The Case Study - the Task `@Test` Methods Explored

I did not create many Task level tests, so there is a lot of scope for increasing coverage here.

The tests don't really reveal any new abstraction features or testing features, but they have helped expand the `TracksApi`.

All the tests here use the `TracksApi` with some bleed over due to use of the REST Assured `Response` object.

The tests cover:

- Create Task.
- Delete Task (indirectly when a Project is deleted).

Supporting Private Methods

You might notice a slight change in the code.

I created some `private` methods to help make the tests more readable.

The fact that I created these methods hints that I might need to refactor the interface of the API class and avoid using the `RestAssured` response, and instead create a `TracksResponse` class with a method to 'get created id'.

Also I tried to make the tests readable by not capturing the `Response` when I make an API call, instead I use the `getLastResponse` method. This might make the test readable in one way, but has forced me to create a `getLastStatusCode` method to make the code more readable.

```
private int getLastStatusCode(TracksApi api) {
    return api.getLastResponse().getStatusCode();
}

private String getIdFromApiResponse(TracksApi api) {
    return new TracksResponseProcessor(
            api.getLastResponse()).getIdFromLocation();
}
```

Create

I wrote a test to create a Task and then assert that the Task is added to the Project.

Points to note:

- Each API call has an assertion after it.
- The test creates a new Project to test against.
- The test adds a new context to the system.
- The test checks that the number of Tasks in the Project increases when a new Task is created.

```
@Test
public void weCanAddTasksToAProject(){

    TracksApi api = new TracksApi(TestEnvDefaults.getTestEnv());

    // create a new project
    api.createProject("A New Project" +
                    new RandomDataGenerator().randomWord());
    Assert.assertEquals(201, getLastStatusCode(api));

    // get the id of the created project
    String createdProjectId = getIdFromApiResponse(api);

    // create a new Context
    api.createContext("context" +
                    new RandomDataGenerator().randomWord());
    Assert.assertEquals(201, getLastStatusCode(api));
```

```
        // get the id of the created context
        String createdContextId = getIdFromApiResponse(api);

        // check task numbers for project
        List<TracksTodo> tasks = api.getProjectTasks(createdProjectId);
        int currentTodos = tasks.size();

        api.createTodo("todo " + new RandomDataGenerator().randomWord(),
                        createdProjectId, createdContextId);
        Assert.assertEquals(201, getLastStatusCode(api));

        // check task numbers increased
        List<TracksTodo> newTasks = api.getProjectTasks(createdProjectId);
        Assert.assertTrue(newTasks.size() > currentTodos);
        Assert.assertTrue(newTasks.size() == currentTodos+1);
    }
```

At first glance, the @Test method could seem reasonable.

- We create the data we want.
- We capture the number of Tasks.
- We assert that the number of Tasks increases.

But..

The @Test method misses out one important assertion.

When we create a Project, surely the first call to getProjectTasks for the Project should return 0 Tasks because we haven't created any yet.

We could easily assert for this.

```
        List<TracksTodo> tasks = api.getProjectTasks(createdProjectId);
        Assert.assertEquals(0, tasks.size());
```

Sadly, this causes the test to fail.

- It might be a bug in the system because the getProjectTasks seems to return all Tasks, even when a specific Project id is asked for.
- This might be the desired behaviour and the documentation should mention this.

Delete

The test is very easy to read, and understand, the scenario flow because of the sequence of API calls. Each API calls is followed by an assertion on status code:

- api.createProject
- api.createContext
- api.createTodo
- api.getTodo
- api.deleteProject
- api.getProject
- api.getTodo

```
@Test
public void whenWeDeleteAProjectTheTasksAreDeletedAsWell(){

    TracksApi api = new TracksApi(TestEnvDefaults.getTestEnv());

    api.createProject("A New Project" +
                    new RandomDataGenerator().randomWord());
    Assert.assertEquals(201, getLastStatusCode(api));
    String createdProjectId = getIdFromApiResponse(api);

    api.createContext("context" +
                    new RandomDataGenerator().randomWord());
    Assert.assertEquals(201, getLastStatusCode(api));
    String createdContextId = getIdFromApiResponse(api);

    api.createTodo("todo " + new RandomDataGenerator().randomWord(),
                createdProjectId, createdContextId);
    Assert.assertEquals(201, getLastStatusCode(api));
    String createdTodoId = getIdFromApiResponse(api);

    api.getTodo(createdTodoId);
    Assert.assertEquals(200, getLastStatusCode(api));

    api.deleteProject(createdProjectId);

    api.getProject(createdProjectId);
```

```
        Assert.assertEquals(404, getLastStatusCode(api));

        // check the todo was deleted as well
        api.getTodo(createdTodoId);
        Assert.assertEquals(404, getLastStatusCode(api));
    }
```

Summary

The tests illustrate that it is very easy to miss defects if we don't add enough assertions into the @Test methods, particularly when we are working with a scenario, or long path through the system states, via multiple API calls.

Private methods are very useful to increase readability for any library interface used. If we find that private methods improve @Test readability and maintainability then we might need to change the library interface, or add an abstraction that exists purely to support the interface readability.

REST Assured JSON and XML Processing

This chapter deviates from the rest of the book, in that I describe code I did not create for the case study.

The case study uses Tracks, but Tracks only uses XML for its REST API. I created additional code to provide an overview of JSON parsing using REST Assured.

In order to make it easier to apply the lessons learned in this book I will describe both JSON and XML processing using REST Assured in this chapter.

Code Example Location

The main code for this section is in the:

- src\test\java folder
- in the restassured package

The code uses two files in the src\test\resources folder:

- xmlexample.xml
  - An XML format file containing XML returned by the Tracks projects list endpoint.
- jsonexample.json
  - A JSON format file, containing the XML converted into JSON to provide an example of the response if the Tracks API supported JSON.

The JSON example test code is in RestAssuredJSONExamplesTest.java and the XML example test code is in RestAssuredXMLExamplesTest.java.

What Is XML?

XML stands for Extensible Markup Language.

It is human readable, and can be very verbose.

XML is a nested set of tags where each tag has an open and closing tag.

e.g. the following represents an id element.

```
<id type="integer">1</id>
```

- tag name is id
- it has an attribute named type which has a string value of "integer"
- the value of the element is 1
- an opening tag is represented by angle brackets <id>
- a closing tag has a / immediately after the < symbol e.g. </id>

In order to be processed by an XML parser it must be well formed, which means every opening tag must have a closing tag and all quotes etc. must be balanced.

You have seen XML throughout the case study in the form of messages returned from Tracks.

e.g. below is an example XML representing the list of projects in Tracks (you can find the full version of this in the xmlexample.xml file in src\test\java\resources)

```
<?xml version="1.0" encoding="UTF-8"?>
<projects type="array">
  <project>
      <id type="integer">1</id>
      <name>A New Projectaniheeiadtatd</name>
      <position type="integer">0</position>
      <description nil="true"/>
      <state>active</state>
      <created-at type="dateTime">2017-06-27T12:25:26+01:00</created-at>
      <updated-at type="dateTime">2017-06-27T12:25:26+01:00</updated-at>
      <default-context-id type="integer" nil="true"/>
      <completed-at type="dateTime" nil="true"/>
      <default-tags nil="true"/>
      <last-reviewed type="dateTime" nil="true"/>
  </project>
</projects>
```

The above list of `projects` has a single `project` in it, and all the fields on a project are listed as separate elements within a `project`.

What Is JSON?

JSON stands for JavaScript Object Notation.

This is real JavaScript code which is also used for representing messages between systems. It is fairly easy to parse and understand.

e.g. the JSON below is a representation of the XML above.

```
{
  "projects": {
    "project": [
      {
        "id":  1,
        "name": "A New Projectaniheeiadtatd",
        "position": 0,
        "description": "",
        "state": "active",
        "created-at": "2017-06-27T12:25:26+01:00",
        "updated-at": "2017-06-27T12:25:26+01:00"
      }
    ]
  }
}
```

- Objects are delineated by opening and closing braces { and }
- Arrays are delineated by open and closing square brackets [and]
- It can be viewed as a hash map with a set of key : value pairs, where the value might be an Integer Literal, String Literal, Object or Array.

In this example we have:

- The whole set of data as an object because of the opening and closing braces as first and last characters.
- A `projects` object.
- An array of `project` objects.
- The fields on the project are represented by a comma separated list of key : value pairs e.g. "id": 1,

REST Assured JSON and XML Parsing

To support this chapter I created a set of 'mock' Tracks endpoints on my web site:

- compendiumdev.co.uk/apps/mocktracks/projectsxml.php[126]
  - returns an XML response with a list of `projects`.
- compendiumdev.co.uk/apps/mocktracks/projectsjson.php[127]
  - returns a JSON response with a list of `projects`.
- compendiumdev.co.uk/apps/mocktracks/reflect.php[128]
  - always returns 200 status code, but the body contains the Verb and the contents of the body sent to the page. Useful to check if the message content you sent is what you expected.

Simple JSON REST Assured Example

A simple JSON REST Assured example is below, this uses the `given`, `when`, `then` style, and asserts using REST Assured

```
String xmlendpoint =
        "http://compendiumdev.co.uk/apps/mocktracks/projectsxml.php";
```

Having defined the endpoint in a `String` variable above, it is possible to `get` the endpoint and then assert that the `body` contains a particular value in the JSON.

```
@Test
public void simpleJSONRestAssuredExample(){

    RestAssured.
        when().
            get(jsonendpoint).
        then().assertThat().
            body("projects.project[0].name",
                equalTo("A New Projectaniheeiadtatd"));
}
```

This will pass when the JSON contains a list of projects where the first project has the name `"A New Projectaniheeiadtatd"`. As represented by the JSON snippet above.

---

[126]http://compendiumdev.co.uk/apps/mocktracks/projectsxml.php
[127]http://compendiumdev.co.uk/apps/mocktracks/projectsjson.php
[128]http://compendiumdev.co.uk/apps/mocktracks/reflect.php

Simple XML REST Assured Example

The equivalent XML REST Assured Example is shown below.

It uses a different end point, i.e. one that returns XML.

```
String xmlendpoint =
        "http://compendiumdev.co.uk/apps/mocktracks/projectsxml.php";
```

But the test is essentially the same:

```
@Test
public void simpleXmlRestAssuredExample(){
    RestAssured.when().get(xmlendpoint).
        then().assertThat().
            body("projects.project[0].name",
                equalTo("A New Projectaniheeiadtatd"));
}
```

REST Assured Parsing

REST Assured uses the `Content-type` header in the response to determine whether to parse the response as XML or as JSON.

The JSON call has a response with a content type header of `application/json` so REST Assured uses the JSON parser.

`Content-Type:application/json`

The XML call has a content type header of `application/xml` in the response so REST Assured uses the XML parser.

It is possible to override the default parsing based on headers, as explained in the official REST Assured documentation[129].

---

[129] https://github.com/rest-assured/rest-assured/wiki/Usage#custom-parsers

GPath

REST Assured uses GPath[130] syntax to access items in the body:

```
"projects.project[0].name"
```

- A . "dot" separated list of tags or object names.
- To access particular values in a list or array use the [n] indexing syntax, which is zero indexed, so [0] is the first item and [1] is the second.

GPath Examples

We can use GPath in the assertThat().body(...) code, and we can chain body calls with and() to check multiple assertions e.g.

```
then().assertThat().
        body("projects.project.size",
                equalTo(6)).and().
        body("projects.project[1].name",
                equalTo("the new name aniheeiaosono")).and().
```

Some examples of GPath:

- projects.project would return the array or list of all project objects.
- projects.project.size() would return the size of the array. When processing JSON I found that I could leave off the () and just use size.
- projects.project[1] would return the second project.
- projects.project[1].name would return the name of the second project.
- projects.project[1].id would return the id of the second project.

We can also use 'filters' with find and findAll e.g.

- projects.project.find {it.id == 3} to return the project with id equal to 3.
- projects.project.findAll {it.id <= 6}.size to return all the projects with id less than or equal to 6. For parsing in XML I found I had to convert the ID to an Integer {it.id.toInteger() <= 6}.

I tend not to use the find and findAll.

---

[130]http://groovy-lang.org/processing-xml.html#_gpath

XML Attributes with GPath

XML tags can have attributes e.g. the id tag in project has a type attribute.

```
<id type="integer">1</id>
```

We can access the attributes using GPath with the @ symbol:

```
Assert.assertEquals("integer",
                xmlPath.get("projects.project[1].id.@type"));
```

JsonPath and XmlPath

As mentioned previously I have a tendency to use REST Assured for HTTP level activities and not for assertion.

Therefore I would normally convert the response into an Object, or parse it with JsonPath, XmlPath, or GSon.

- JsonPath is a REST Assured supplied library for parsing JSON
- XmlPath is a REST Assured library for parsing XML
- GSon is a Google library for parsing JSON

JsonPath and XmlPath use the GPath syntax as described earlier for the body assertions.

If I wanted to use REST Assured to make the HTTP call and then use JsonPath to parse the result I might do something like the following:

```
Response response = RestAssured.
        when().
        get(jsonendpoint).
        andReturn();
```

You saw me use the Response object in the case study code.

I would then convert the body of the Response to a String and parse it into a JsonPath object.

```
JsonPath jsonPath = new JsonPath(response.body().asString());
```

I can then use the `JsonPath` object to `get` the fields and values using GPath format queries, the following returns a `List` of `HashMap` objects:

```
List<HashMap<String,String>> ret = jsonPath.get("projects.project");
Assert.assertEquals(6, ret.size());
```

I can use the `HashMap` to access the field values.

```
Assert.assertEquals("A New Projectaniheeiadtatd",
                    ret.get(0).get("name"));
```

Only the JsonPath returns a HashMap. A related method on XmlPath is `getList` which returns a `List` of `Strings`:

```
XmlPath xmlPath = new XmlPath(response.body().asString());

List ret = xmlPath.getList("projects.project");
Assert.assertEquals(6, ret.size());
```

You saw from the earlier code that I prefer to work with the `getNodeChildren` method, rather than `getList` when working with XmlPath.

The source code contains examples of using JsonPath and XmlPath to get various portions of the returned XML and JSON.

Parsing from File or String

Both JsonPath and XmlPath can be instantiated using String or File contents.

I used `String` in the previous examples when I converted the `Response` body to a `String`.

The `@Test` methods also have examples using files:

```
File jsonExample = new File(System.getProperty("user.dir"),
        "src/test/resources/jsonxml/jsonexample.json");

JsonPath jsonPath = new JsonPath(jsonExample);
```

Once we have a JsonPath or XmlPath object it doesn't matter how it was instantiated, we can still use the various get methods to retrieve data from the JSON or XML.

Parsing from URI

Both JsonPath and XmlPath have the ability to be instantiated with a URI.

In this case, JsonPath or XmlPath will make an HTTP call to the URI and instantiate itself from the returned body.

e.g.

```
URI endpoint = new URI(xmlendpoint);

ProjectFromXmlOrJson projectFromXml;
projectFromXml = new XmlPath(endpoint).
                    getObject("projects.project[1]",
                            ProjectFromXmlOrJson.class);

Assert.assertEquals(3, projectFromXml.id);
```

Deserialization to Objects

Deserialization basically means converting a String (or series of bytes) into an instantiated Object. It is also known as unmarshalling.

The most strategic approach to parsing JSON or XML is to deserialize it into a plain old Java object. This allows your abstraction layers to return objects that the test code can use. The test code then does not have to concern itself with JSON, XML or the HTTP abstractions.

For JSON this usually requires a simple Java object to represent the message content e.g. the following code represents the data in the project element:

```
public class ProjectJson {
    public int id;
    public String name;
    public int position;
    public String description;
    public String state;
    public Date created_at;
    public Date updated_at;
    public int default_context;
    public Date completed_at;
    public String default_tags;
    public Date last_reviewed;
}
```

To convert a Response to a ProjectJson class we can either use getObject on an instantiated JsonPath object.

```
ProjectJson theProjectFromJson =
                    jsonPath.getObject(
                            "projects.project[1]",
                            ProjectJson.class);
Assert.assertEquals(3, theProjectFromJson.id);
```

Or we could getObject from the RestAssured usage:

```
ProjectJson projectFromJson = RestAssured.
        when().
        get(jsonendpoint).
        jsonPath().
        getObject("projects.project[1]", ProjectJson.class);

Assert.assertEquals(3, projectFromJson.id);
```

To deserialize from XML we may need to annotate the Java object fields to map them to the tag names in the XML. Because the XML tags can use '-' but the Java fields use '_' e.g.

```
@XmlElement(name="created-at")
public Date created_at;
```

And you can see this in the context of the full class below:

```java
public class ProjectFromXmlOrJson {
    public int id;
    public String name;
    public int position;
    public String description;
    public String state;
    @XmlElement(name="created-at")
    public Date created_at;
    @XmlElement(name="updated-at")
    public Date updated_at;
    @XmlElement(name="default-context")
    public int default_context;
    @XmlElement(name="completed-at")
    public Date completed_at;
    @XmlElement(name="default-tags")
    public String default_tags;
    @XmlElement(name="last-reviewed")
    public Date last_reviewed;
}
```

Even though the object is annotated for XML usage, I could use the object for JSON deserialization without amendment.

The XML deserialization will work without requiring any new Dependencies. The JSON deserialization requires GSon being added as a dependency in the pom.xml

```xml
<dependency>
    <groupId>com.google.code.gson</groupId>
    <artifactId>gson</artifactId>
    <version>2.8.1</version>
</dependency>
```

In addition to deserializing to objects, we very often send messages over REST where the payload (or message body) is a serialized object, rather than using templates for all our messages.

Deserialization in Practice

To offer an example of how deserialization can help, we will have a look at the getProjects method which I originally used in the case study.

```java
public List<TracksProject> getProjects() {

    List<TracksProject> projects = new ArrayList<>();

    Response projectsListResponse=
                    httpMessageSender.getXMLResponseFrom(
                                    TracksApiEndPoints.projects);

    String xml = projectsListResponse.body().asString();

    XmlPath xmlPath = new XmlPath(xml);
    NodeChildren nodes = xmlPath.getNodeChildren("projects.project");

    for(Node contextNode : nodes.list()){

        TracksProject project = new TracksProject();

        for(Node element : contextNode.children().list()){

            project.setKeyValuePair(element.name(), element.value());
        }
        projects.add(project);
    }

    return projects;
}
```

The code above:

- Calls the projects end point to return the XML example we have been using in this chapter.
- Uses XmlPath to get the projects using GPath.
- Uses the getNodeChildren and iterates over this to create a list of TracksProject.
- The TracksProject isn't a 'real' object and is crudely created from a HashMap.

It would have been far better if I had deserialized the project XML into an object and created a list.

The following method does exactly that. It can be found in the SerializingApi class in the restassured.api package in src\test\java.

```
public List<ProjectFromXmlOrJson> getProjects(){

    List<ProjectFromXmlOrJson> projects = new ArrayList<>();

    String xml = RestAssured.
            when().get(xmlendpoint).
            andReturn().body().asString();

    XmlPath xmlPath = new XmlPath(xml);

    projects = xmlPath.getList("projects.project",
                    ProjectFromXmlOrJson.class);

    return projects;
}
```

The above:

- Makes a call to the API.
- Uses GPath to select the list of `project` elements.
- Finally deserializes the list using `getList`, where each item in the list is an instantiated `ProjectFromXmlOrJson` object.

I initially used `getObject` to do this, by finding the number of projects and iterating over each to deserialize them individually. But it seemed easier to use the single call to `getList` rather than the iteration code shown below:

```
int numberOfProjects =
            xmlPath.getInt("projects.project.size()");
for(int projectIndex=0;
            projectIndex<numberOfProjects;
                    projectIndex++){

    String query = String.format(
                        "projects.project[%d]",
                        projectIndex);

    ProjectFromXmlOrJson project;

    project = xmlPath.getObject(query,
```

```
                                    ProjectFromXmlOrJson.class);

        projects.add(project);
    }
```

In its current form the @Test code to use the new API call looks as follows:

```
@Test
public void anXmlAPIDeserializationExample(){

    List<ProjectFromXmlOrJson> projects;

    projects = new SerializingApi(xmlendpoint).getProjects();

    Assert.assertEquals(6, projects.size());
    Assert.assertEquals(1, projects.get(0).id);
    Assert.assertEquals("A New Projectaniheeiadtatd",
                        projects.get(0).name);
}
```

I think this approach is easier to extend and maintain because we only change the class we deserialize into, rather than the API method.

Also, it increases the separation of abstraction layers so the @Test method is less likely to need to know about the API.

Very often we don't pull out portions of a response (i.e. just the project). Instead we often have an object that represents the full response payload, then we can deserialize the whole response into an object with getObject.

Serialization in Practice

Serialization basically means to convert an Object into a String (or series of bytes), suitable for writing to file or sending in messages. It is also known as marshalling.

It is common when automating APIs to serialize objects into request payloads, rather than using string templates.

The case study code used string templates e.g. the case study createTodo API method:

```
public Response createTodo(String todoName, String projectId, String contextId) {
    String msg = String.format("<todo>\n<description>%s</description>\n" +
                "   <project_id>%s</project_id>\n" +
                "   <context_id>%s</context_id>\n" +
                "</todo>",
            todoName, projectId, contextId);

    Response response= httpMessageSender.postXmlMessageTo(msg,
                                        TracksApiEndPoints.todos);
    return response;
}
```

A more strategic approach would involve:

- Create a payload object.
- Use REST Assured to serialize the object during the sending of the message.

Since Tracks uses XML I would create a todo payload object like:

```
@XmlRootElement(name="todo")
public class SerializedTodo {
    public String description;
    public String project_id;
    public String context_id;

    public SerializedTodo(String todoName, String projectId, String contextId){
        this.description = todoName;
        this.project_id = projectId;
        this.context_id= contextId;
    }

    public SerializedTodo(){}
}
```

The API call using this looks as follows:

```
public Response createTodo(SerializedTodo todo) {
    return RestAssured.
            given().
                contentType(ContentType.XML).
                body(todo).
            when().
                post(xmlendpoint);
}
```

The following @Test demonstrate this approach:

```
@Test
public void anXmlAPISerializationExample(){

    String reflectEndPoint =
            "http://compendiumdev.co.uk/apps/mocktracks/reflect.php";

    String todoName = "todo " + new RandomDataGenerator().randomWord();

    SerializedTodo todo;
    todo =  new SerializedTodo(todoName, "12", "13");

    SerializingApi api = new SerializingApi(reflectEndPoint);
    Response response = api.createTodo(todo);

    System.out.println(response.body().asString());
}
```

When run, this printed the following (I edited it for formatting):

```
POST
<?xml version="1.0" encoding="ISO-8859-1" standalone="yes"?>
<todo>
    <description>todo anihrsairiarh</description>
    <project_id>12</project_id>
    <context_id>13</context_id>
</todo>
```

If I change the contentType value in the API call from XML to JSON i.e. content-Type(ContentType.JSON). then the payload is converted to JSON rather than XML.

```
POST
{
  "description":"todo anihrsdoaooee",
  "project_id":"12",
  "context_id":"13"
}
```

This makes supporting an API that uses both JSON and XML quite simple. All we do is switch the contentType from ContentType.JSON to ContentType.XML.

More Information

The REST Assured Usage Documentation covers GPath and deserialization pretty well and should be your first reference point when working with REST Assured.

- REST Assured Usage Documentation[131]

I also found the following references useful:

- A JsonPath blog post on the Jayway web site[132]
- Deserialization Usage Section[133]
- JSON parsing Usage[134]
- JsonPath[135]
- GPath[136]

More examples of serialized objects for JSON messages can be found in Mark Winteringham's api-framework project on GitHub:

- api-framework REST Assured example[137]

[131] https://github.com/rest-assured/rest-assured/wiki/Usage

[132] https://blog.jayway.com/2013/04/12/whats-new-in-rest-assured-1-8/

[133] https://github.com/rest-assured/rest-assured/wiki/Usage#deserialization

[134] https://github.com/rest-assured/rest-assured/wiki/Usage#json-example

[135] https://github.com/rest-assured/rest-assured/wiki/Usage#json-using-jsonpath

[136] http://groovy-lang.org/processing-xml.html#_gpath

[137] https://github.com/mwinteringham/api-framework/tree/master/java/restassured

Summary

I did not need to parse JSON in the case study so the examples use XmlPath. The use of JsonPath and XmlPath is very similar. In fact the JsonPath is often easier than parsing XmlPath.

Code for all these examples is in the source that you can download to support the book from GitHub[138]. You can find it in the `src\test java` folder and the `restassured` package.

For long term strategic automating, we normally deserialize messages into objects as it makes it easier to maintain and refactor code. We also gain the ability to maintain more of a separation between the REST messages and asserting on values in the messages. Assertions would tend to use the deserialized objects, rather than GPath on the returned `Response` objects.

---

[138] https://github.com/eviltester/tracksrestcasestudy

Summary of REST Assured

REST Assured has been described over the last few chapters. Since the description of its functionality has been spread out, this chapter will collate the main information into a short summary.

The main web sites for REST Assured are:

- rest-assured.io[139]
- github.com/rest-assured/rest-assured[140]

Make sure you read the REST Assured Usage Documentation for more information as the examples in this book do not cover the full functionality of REST Assured.

- REST Assured Usage Documentation[141]

Adding REST Assured with Maven

Add REST Assured in your Maven pom.xml file as a dependency:

```
<dependency>
    <groupId>io.rest-assured</groupId>
    <artifactId>rest-assured</artifactId>
    <version>3.0.1</version>
</dependency>
```

Setting a Proxy for REST Assured

The proxy method is public and accessed statically so can be called on RestAssured at any time.

---

[139] http://rest-assured.io

[140] https://github.com/rest-assured/rest-assured

[141] https://github.com/rest-assured/rest-assured/wiki/Usage

```
RestAssured.proxy(proxyURL, proxyPort);
```

You can also set the proxy using the Java virtual machine proxy configuration.

```
-Dhttp.proxyHost=localhost -Dhttp.proxyPort=8080
```

Sending Message with REST Assured

Use the `given, when, then` syntax of REST Assured to send a message:

```
given().
        contentType("text/xml").
when().
        get("http://192.168.17.129/todos.xml").
then().
        statusCode(401);
```

given, when, then

The `given, when, then` methods help partition the call into different sections:

- `given`, setup all the message details that you need.
- `when`, issue the type of message.
- `then`, assert on message details and/or return the response.

Using `given` to Set the Message Details

We use the `given` section to configure the message e.g. configure the `content-type` header:

```
given().
        contentType("text/xml").
```

In the case study code we use the `given` section to configure

- Content type of the message.

- Basic Authentication header.
- General header configuration.
- The body text of the message.
- Cookies to be included in the request headers.

We use the `when` section to:

- Send a message either with `post`, `delete`, `get` or `put`.

The `then` section is used for:

- Asserting on values in the response.
- Returning the response.
- Return parts of the response.

Configure Content Type

REST Assured has the `contentType` method to set the `content-type` header.

```
contentType("text/xml").
```

Also:

```
contentType("text/html,application/xhtml+xml," +
            "application/xml;q=0.9,*/*;q=0.8").
```

You could also use the general `header` method and use `content-type` as the header name.

- Content Type Documentation[142]

It is also possible to use `contentType` in REST Assured for message serialisation and asserting the response content type.

- Content Type based serialisation Documentation[143]
- Assert on Content Type Documentation[144]

---

[142]https://github.com/rest-assured/rest-assured/wiki/usage#content-type

[143]https://github.com/rest-assured/rest-assured/wiki/usage#content-type-based-serialization

[144]https://github.com/rest-assured/rest-assured/wiki/usage#content-type-1

Configure Basic Authentication

The `Tracks` API uses Basic Authentication and REST Assured has a high level method to let us configure that easily - `auth`

```
auth().preemptive().basic("user", "bitnami").
```

I use `preemptive` to force the sending of a single message.

- REST Assured Authentication Documentation[145]

Configure a Header on the Message

Set a `header` using a name value pair as the parameters.

```
header(new Header("Authorization", "Basic dXNlcjpiaXRuYW1p")).
```

- REST Assured headers Documentation[146]

Set the Body Text of the HTTP Message

We can set the body of the message with a single method:

```
body(msg).
```

- Set Request Body Documentation[147]

You can also use `param` and `formParam` to set parameters as a message body:

- `param` Documentation[148]

Set the Cookies

To set the cookies, use a `Map<String,String>`

---

[145]https://github.com/rest-assured/rest-assured/wiki/usage#authentication
[146]https://github.com/rest-assured/rest-assured/wiki/usage#headers
[147]https://github.com/rest-assured/rest-assured/wiki/usage#request-body
[148]https://github.com/rest-assured/rest-assured/wiki/usage#parameters

```
private HashMap<String,String> anEmptyCookieJar(){
    return new HashMap<String,String>();
}
```

Then include that `Map` in the message with `cookies` and REST Assured will create the `cookie` header in the request:

```
cookies(cookieJar).
```

- Cookies Documentation[149]

Using when to Make HTTP Requests

`post`, `get`, `put` and `delete` all have similar syntax and take the `url` to call as the parameter. The case study used `when` explicitly for `post` and `put`, and implicitly for `get` and `delete`. e.g.

- Explicitly for `post` and `put`:

```
when().
        post(theEndPointUrl.toExternalForm()).
```

- Implicitly for `get` and `delete`:

```
given().
    auth().preemptive().
                basic(authUser, authPassword).
    cookies(cookieJar).
    contentType(ct).
delete(theEndPointUrl.toExternalForm()).
```

Any of the methods; `post`, `get`, `put` and `delete`, can be used as implicit `when` blocks, or explicitly after a `when()` method call.

- Invoking HTTP Resources[150]

---

[149] https://github.com/rest-assured/rest-assured/wiki/usage#cookies

[150] https://github.com/rest-assured/rest-assured/wiki/usage#invoking-http-resources

Using then to Process Response

In the code you'll see that I primarily assert on status codes:

```
then().
        statusCode(401);
```

And I return the response for later processing. I primarily do this with an 'implicit' then, i.e. I don't write the then().

```
andReturn();
```

But in my version 2.2.0 usage I did use the then() block to extract a response:

```
Response projectsHtml = when().get(aUrl).
                        then().extract().response();
```

I tend to return the Response and then use the Response methods to assert and extract information, but REST Assured supports many different methods of asserting and extracting values from the request:

- Getting Response Data Documentation[151]

Basic Example

A pretty good example of much of the above is shown below:

---

[151]https://github.com/rest-assured/rest-assured/wiki/usage#getting-response-data

```
Response ret =
        given().
                auth().preemptive().
                    basic(authUser, authPassword).
                body(msg).
                contentType(contentType).
                cookies(cookieJar).
        when().
                post(theEndPointUrl.toExternalForm()).
        andReturn();
```

Assertions Using body in then

We can use REST Assured to assert on values in the message.

```
RestAssured.when().get(xmlendpoint).
    then().assertThat().
        body("projects.project[0].name",
            equalTo("A New Projectaniheeiadtatd"));
```

The selection of elements from the body uses GPath[152].

In GPath:

- The query elements are separated by .
- Arrays use the [n] notation where [0] is the first item and [-1] is the last.
- @ can be used to return attributes from XML.
- Groovy can be used in the filter e.g. methods like .size() and toInteger().

The content-type header of the response is used to determine the parsing, unless over-ridden by the programmer[153].

---

[152]http://groovy-lang.org/processing-xml.html#_gpath

[153]https://github.com/rest-assured/rest-assured/wiki/Usage#custom-parsers

JsonPath and XmlPath

The response can be processed as JSON with JsonPath or XML with XmlPath. These are REST Assured libraries that can be used independently of REST Assured.

They can be instantiated from a `String`, or read from a `File`. They can even take a URI object and make HTTP requests directly.

The `get` methods can be used to return integers, strings or lists of data based on the GPath query used.

Serialization and Deserialization

We can use REST Assured to build objects by deserialization of data returned via GPath directly into a class:

Deserialize a `List` of objects:

```
projects = xmlPath.getList("projects.project",
                ProjectFromXmlOrJson.class);
```

Deserialize a single object:

```
getObject("projects.project[1]",
            ProjectFromXmlOrJson.class);
```

When deserializing from XML we may need to annotate fields in the class we want to deserialize to if we want to change names of fields:

```
@XmlElement(name="created-at")
public Date created_at;
```

To deserialize JSON we need to add GSon as a dependency in the `pom.xml`.

Rather than build up message bodies with `String` templates we could serialize an object to create the body of the message. We serialize to JSON or XML depending on the chosen `contentType`.

```
given().
    contentType(ContentType.XML).
    body(todo).
when().
    post(xmlendpoint);
```

Summary

REST Assured is a very extensive library and we have barely scratched the surface of it in this case study.

Were I to rely on it further I can see a lot of value in:

- ResponseSpecBuilder[154] to create a reusable given
- Path Arguments[155] to configure requests more easily
- Session Configuration[156]

It is worth reading through the documentation because REST Assured can handle most of the situations you will encounter when automating REST interfaces.

References

Full documentation:

- REST Assured Usage Documentation[157]

Specific Sections:

- Content Type[158]
- REST Assured Authentication[159]

---

[154] https://github.com/rest-assured/rest-assured/wiki/usage#specification-re-use

[155] https://github.com/rest-assured/rest-assured/wiki/usage#path-arguments

[156] https://github.com/rest-assured/rest-assured/wiki/usage#session-support

[157] https://github.com/rest-assured/rest-assured/wiki/Usage

[158] https://github.com/rest-assured/rest-assured/wiki/usage#content-type

[159] https://github.com/rest-assured/rest-assured/wiki/usage#authentication

Suggested Exercises

There is still plenty of work to do on this code base. Therefore it offers a good set of exercise potential. Either to work:

- on your own,
- for a half day team exploration,
- or for an on-site interactive workshop (you can contact the author[160] for details of face to face training).

Installation Exercises

- Get Tracks Installed (recommend you use a virtual machine).
- Install the tools.
- Try the code in the book using the tools.
- Use cURL to access the API.
- Use Postman to access the API.
- Feed cURL and Postman through Proxy tools.
- Run the existing test code against Tracks.
- Run the existing test code against Tracks through a Proxy.

Coding Exercises

I'm going to suggest a few high level objectives in this chapter which you might want to use as exercises. To expand the current @Test method code, and supporting abstractions to cover: authentication, projects, tasks, contexts, API coverage, outstanding TODO items in the code.

---

[160]http://www.compendiumdev.co.uk/page/contact_us

Authentication

- Explorae combinations of requests with valid/invalid basic authentication headers, content headers and handle any content returned in the responses.

Project:

- Move `Project` into different status - active, hidden, status.
- Check field value validation for `Project` creation and amendment e.g. invalid Project names, special characters, blank names, long names, etc.

Tasks:

- Delete an individual Task.
- Amend fields on a Task.
- Field validation on creation and amendment.
- Amend Tasks to be 'done', access the 'done' API to check.

Contexts:

- Read Contexts via the API.
- Create, amend and delete Contexts via the API.

API:

- Look through the API documentation `/integrations/rest_api:`
  - assert on any requirements listed,
  - cover any API endpoints that are not yet used in the `@Test` code.

You could also convert the API to use serialization and deserialization to increase the flexibility of testing and improve the API code.

TODO Items:

- Look through the source code and find any of the outstanding TODOs left in the code, then amend the code to implement those you find.

Refactor and Expand

The next chapter lists some refactoring ideas, and you might have to perform some refactoring to allow you to try these next exercise ideas:

- Replace REST Assured with one of the other Java HTTP libraries e.g. Unirest, or Java HTTP Client.
- Use a different assertion library and see if it lets you write the `@Test` code in a more readable way e.g. AssertJ.

Summary

- Basic (repeat the case study)
  - Download the VM.
  - Try the tools.
  - Use the Postman collection.
  - etc.
- Moderate:
  - Expand the coverage.
  - Refactor the code.
  - Add error handling.
  - Fix some of the TODOs.
- Advanced:
  - Use a different HTTP library.

I did not provide any 'answers' to the above exercise suggestions because you can use the existing code as a basis for all of the suggestions. And it is important that you experiment to find your own coding and implementation style.

If you encounter any 'bugs' when automating then make sure you can recreate the issue interactively with cURL or Postman to do your best to ensure that you have found a system issue rather than a problem with your automating.

Feel free to look through the existing `@Test` methods and when you identify gaps, write an `@Test` method to cover the gap.

The next chapter will describe refactoring that you might want to undertake as an additional exercise.

Future Refactoring

Since the case study was based on 'actual' code, there were coding, and design choices that could have been improved.

This chapter looks at a few of these in more detail.

The changes described below are not 'TODO' items, they are actions that I could take to make the code:

- cleaner,
- easier to maintain,
- better designed.

Very often I write code that works, and then spend time later making the code better.

Instead of Returning a Response Object

In the TracksApi we saw that the RestAssured library was still tightly coupled to the TracksApi due to some of the TracksApi methods returning a RestAssured Response object.

To create a proper separation we would need to have the TracksApi methods return a TracksResponse object e.g.

```
public TracksResponse createContext(String aContext) {

    String tmplt = "<context><name>%s</name></context>";

    String msg = String.format(tmplt, aContext);

    Response response = httpMessageSender.postXmlMessageTo(msg,
            TracksApiEndPoints.contexts);

    return new TracksResponse(response);
}
```

This would support the access to the HTTP response required by the @Test code and could be expanded if required in the future.

```java
public class TracksResponse {

    private final int statusCode;
    private final String body;
    private final Map<String,String> responseHeaders;

    public TracksResponse(Response response) {
        this.statusCode = response.getStatusCode();

        this.responseHeaders = new HashMap<>();
        Headers headers = response.getHeaders();
        for(Header header: headers){
            responseHeaders.put(header.getName(), header.getValue());
        }

        this.body = response.body().asString();
    }

    public int getStatusCode(){
        return statusCode;
    }

    public String body(){
        return body;
    }

    public Map<String,String> getHeaders(){
        return responseHeaders;
    }
}
```

Ultimately this would mean that the we would find it easier to use a different HttpMessageSender implementation e.g. we might choose to re-implement the HttpMessageSender using HttpClient instead of RestAssured and our @Test methods would not require any amendment.

This would enforce the logical split that the TracksApi and the HttpMessageSender imply exists.

Refactoring to a `TracksResponse`

If we immediately changed all the code from `Response` to `TracksResponse` then we would have to make quite a lot of change very quickly.

And that can introduce risk into our process.

An alternative approach is to have the `TracksResponse` class `implement Response`. Then we can gradually amend the code to return `TracksResponse` objects instead of `Response` objects and we don't have to implement the change in one sweeping code amendment.

Since the `TracksResponse` really only needs to implement three methods to support our current `@Test` methods. We would make the `TracksResponse` implementation for every other method on `Response` throw a `RuntimeException`. This way we would be alerted to any new methods we had to implement in `TracksResponse` and would have an obvious indicator that the method needs to be implemented or we implement the client functionality with the existing three methods.

What Would You Do?

I suggest that you:

- Download the code.
- Run it against the Tracks API.
- Review the code.
- Make a list of your own refactorings.

You can build the list by looking:

- For what confuses you.
  - Perhaps you could refactor the code to make it easier to read.
- For what annoys you.
  - Be careful about refactoring for style though, since 'style' is a very subjective evaluation.
- To remove duplication.
  - The code hasn't been written with shared code in mind, so there are probably patterns of behaviour you could extract out, or repeated code that deserves its own class.

When you refactor:

- If possible, add Unit tests around the code prior to refactoring.
- Certainly, add Unit tests around the code when you refactor as 'extract to class'.

Refactoring Resources

Recommended books:

- Refactoring by Martin Fowler
    - martinfowler.com/books/refactoring.html[161]
- Working Effectively with Legacy Code by Michael Feathers
    - Michael's company book page
        * r7krecon.com/legacy-code[162]
    - Michael Feather's Blog
        * michaelfeathers.silvrback.com[163]

Recommended Web Sites:

- refactoring.com[164] has an on-line catalogue of refactorings

Summary

Refactoring can make code cleaner, easier to maintain and better designed.

Refactoring really means changing the implementation of the code but not its external interface.

To help enforce that, and make sure we don't make mistakes during refactoring, we can use the automated refactoring features in our IDE, and add Unit tests into our code.

---

[161] http://www.martinfowler.com/books/refactoring.html
[162] http://www.r7krecon.com/legacy-code
[163] https://michaelfeathers.silvrback.com/
[164] http://www.refactoring.com

Conclusions and Summary

I hope this text has helped. I covered a lot of material in this book, partly by covering it at a high level, but pretty much all of it has been supported by actual working code.

Next Steps

For next steps, if you haven't already:

- Read the code on GitHub.
- Install Tracks in a VM or locally.
- Start working with the API using the tools mentioned:
    - cURL,
    - Postman,
    - REST Assured.
- Try running the code from the case study.
- Work through the exercises to expand the coverage of the API.
- Refactor the code to make it your own.

Reminder of the Non-Obvious

Some of the information covered has been fairly obvious, but supported with actual code to make it add value:

- How to use cURL
- How to use the tools, etc.

I think you'll see information in this case study that you won't see in many other places:

- App as API.
- REST Assured wrapped with abstractions.

- Test Data creation through web scraping.
- Random Test Data Creation.
- Extensive Abstraction creation.

I use all of the above on production projects.

App as API

The concept of "App as API" started, for me, when I had to work with production systems that were simply "not automatable", or at least that was what I was told, and what I initially thought.

I created the "App as API" concept as a way of creating workarounds for impossible to automate applications like:

- Combine GUI with API at a high level of abstraction so the @Test code doesn't care how we implemented the action.
- Capture messages that the GUI sends and convert them to templates so you can resend them easily.
- 'steal' cookies from a GUI session and then add them to future HTTP messages to skip application flows and GUI screens.

Essentially, do whatever you have to do, to automate the application to support your ability to test.

Be aware that every, shortcut, or workaround, that you take adds risk e.g.

- When templating GUI HTTP messages, there is a risk that the GUI changes and sends different messages, but you haven't updated your templates.
    - When they fail, you just update them.
    - If they don't fail, then you cease to test the application as currently written and have introduced false confidence in the automated coverage.

You are modelling the application at a very physical level, therefore you are very vulnerable to application changes, and you might need to mitigate against that.

Also when the @Test should care if it uses the API, then we use a lower level of abstraction. e.g. drop down to use REST Assured to make HTTP calls directly.

The point behind the abstraction code is that it works at the level we need it to, and we are not constrained to one level of abstraction - create as many abstraction models that you need.

REST Assured Wrapped with Abstractions

Just because you are using a library or a tool does not mean that you have to use every feature of that tool or library.

I didn't use many of the REST Assured features simply because I wanted to model the `@Test` code in a way that supported more use cases than using REST Assured directly would support.

If I had used the `given`, `when`, `then` etc. in my `@Test` code, it would have been harder for me to re-use the code I'd written to support adhoc exploration or adhoc data driven coverage.

By creating an abstraction layer to sit on top of REST Assured, I was able to create re-usable and easy to read code that supported both: ongoing automated assertions within continuous integration, and adhoc exploration.

Also note, that some of the `@Test` methods did use REST Assured in a very low level manner because REST Assured was the right level of abstraction to model those `@Test` methods.

Test Data Creation Through Web Scraping

In the case study I used data created by someone else. But I have used this on production projects by scraping data from our own production systems to use in testing.

This can give me data that is appropriate for the environment I work in, and is often easier than writing conversion routines from CMS systems or the systems that users enter data into.

Random Test Data Creation

Many people do not like to use Random Data when they automate applications.

I often use random data.

I take the view that if the data comes from an 'equivalence class' then I can automate it because that might expose an error in my modelling e.g perhaps the equivalence classes are not as equivalent as I think they are.

Other people take the view that, we should not need to randomly create data because our test code should be designed to cover what we need. That is valid, but, since I know that I can introduce bugs into my test derivation, as well as my production code, I like to use every tool at my disposal to increase variety in my testing. Random data is an easy way to introduce variation into your testing.

Still, other people take the view that random data can be a source of intermittent execution and that an `@Test` method might fail on one run, but pass next time because of different data. That might be true. If it is true, then it means we have made a mistake with our data modelling and random data creation because we should not be generating data that causes a particular test to exercise different functional flows (unless that is what we want to do). Rather than avoid random data, I would fix the data creation so that it does what we want.

Extensive Abstraction Creation

Even though we automated very few functional flows through the application with the `@Test` methods, we do have a lot of abstraction layers to support the code.

This is partly due to the nature of the code - it was written to demonstrate approaches. But, also because I refactor my `@Test` methods continuously to:

- make them more readable,
- make them easier to maintain.

This has the side-effect that:

- I create abstraction layers as I go.
- I can re-use my abstraction layers to support exploration.

I can't stress enough how valuable it is to be able to interactively explore the application and conduct exploratory testing from within the IDE by writing code.

Many people have:

- a suite of automated tests for the API,
- manual testing of the API using a GUI tool.

But with no overlap between them.

This means repeating work that has already been successfully completed for the API layers and automated test code, to create the same messages in the GUI tools.

This might help expose more defects because of an increased variety in the message generation approaches, but it might also waste time due to inefficiency.

I like my work in automating to support my work in exploratory testing.

I have helped clients build abstraction layers to support their exploratory testing that they have subsequently gone on to use to automate the REST APIs as part of continuous integration.

Summary

The code for the case study was written over an elapsed time of a couple of years, but I think it represents about one to two weeks work of a single person. Imagine someone who was performing exploratory testing, coding automated execution, raising defects, and responding to application version changes.

As such, I think it offers a good sized body of code for future study and particularly for experimentation.

I suggest that you can use this to really push your learning of API testing and automated code maintenance by expanding the automated coverage with new `@Test` methods and by refactoring the code.

Appendix - Random Data Creation for v 2.3.0 Testing

For version 2.3.0 testing I wanted a self contained approach for creating test data.

The code for the Random Data Creation is in:

- src\main\java
- with the root package hierarchy
    - package api.version_2_3_0.testdata

As background, this is test data for interactive testing i.e. people exploring the REST API with cURL, Postman and their initial tentative automating of the REST API.

The data had to support human readability.

Unlike the test data generation in the main API test code which just has to support uniqueness.

The RandomDataGenerator supports uniqueness - assuming it is only called once per millisecond.

```java
public class RandomDataGenerator {
    public String randomWord() {
        return String.valueOf(System.currentTimeMillis()).
                replaceAll("1", "a").
                replaceAll("2", "d").
                replaceAll("3", "o").
                replaceAll("4", "n").
                replaceAll("5", "e").
                replaceAll("6", "r").
                replaceAll("7", "t").
                replaceAll("8", "h").
                replaceAll("9", "i").
                replaceAll("0", "s");
    }
}
```

But it doesn't necessarily create very readable names.

e.g.

- Projectanhdnanhhoeoe
- Projectanhdnanhhoeot
- Projectanhdnanhhoeor

I needed a different random data generator.

For version 2.2.0 testing I took the decision to 'scrape' similar domain data from a public Wunderlist web page. When it came time to test 2.3.0, Wunderlist had deleted that page and the option was no longer available - which was probably for the best since it was probably copyrighted to Wunderlist anyway.

I wanted something simple to write, but which generated readable and valid data.

I created a simple symbol replacement system.

Symbol Replacement

If I have a string e.g.:

- "gv cfn"

I could parse that string to find the symbols in it:

- "gv"
- "cfn"

Say I also had a list of Generic Verbs:

e.g. "buy", "find", "purchase"

And a list of Common Food names:

e.g. "pie", "Pudding", "stew"

Then, if I replaced "gv" with a random word from my list of Generic Verbs, and I replaced "cfn" with a random word from my list of Common Food Names, I could generate a small set of random two word sentences:

- "buy pie"
- "find pie"
- "purchase pudding"
- "buy stew"
- "purchase pie"
- "find pudding"
- "purchase stew"
- "buy pudding"
- "find stew"

This is the basic approach I took for generating the data. Hence why you'll see it referred to as a Food Backed Data Retriever:

- RandomFoodBackedDataRetriever

Interface TestDataRetriever

When I started writing the Test Data Generator I wasn't sure how I was going to do it, but I knew that I wanted to have two basic functions:

- Create data for Projects.
- Create data for TODOs for a Project.

I wrote an interface that would give me freedom to try different implementations:

```
public interface TestDataRetriever {
    List<Project> getProjects();

    List<Todo> getTodosForProject(String anID);
}
```

In the end it turned out that I didn't need to pass in the projectId for the TODOs, but I never made time to fix it, so this is technical debt.

RandomFoodBackedDataRetriever

The RandomFoodBackedDataRetriever is not a large class but I'll explore it in small chunks.

First we declare the class as an implementer of the TestDataRetriever interface, this makes it easier to use different data generators at a later date, assuming that we code to the interface rather than the concrete class.

```
public class RandomFoodBackedDataRetriever
                        implements TestDataRetriever {
```

The declaration section defines the constants and fields in use:

```
private final String [] projectNameSentences =
                            {"gv cfn", "gv cu"};
private final String [] todoNameSentences =
                            {"gv cu", "gv fn", "gv vn",
                             "fpv fn", "fpv fn", "fpv vn"};
private Random r;

public static final int MINIMUM_NUMBER_OF_PROJECTS = 10;
public static final int MAXIMUM_NUMBER_OF_PROJECTS = 100;

public static final int MINIMUM_NUMBER_OF_TODOS = 3;
public static final int MAXIMUM_NUMBER_OF_TODOS = 20;
```

In the above we have created replacement templates for the Projects and TODOs. We will look at what "gv cfn" maps on to in just a few moments.

Constants represent the minimum and maximum numbers of entities we will create. In theory this could be set or overridden when the generator is constructed, but at this point they are constants.

```
public RandomFoodBackedDataRetriever(){
    this.r = new Random();
}
```

The constructor above simply instantiates the random value generator that we will use in the body of the class.

getProjects **and** getTodosForProject

Both of the methods which generate Projects and TODOs have the same format. So we will
mainly look a the getProjects here.

```java
public List<Project> getProjects(){

    List<String> projectNames;

    projectNames = getRandomListFrom(projectNameSentences,
            MINIMUM_NUMBER_OF_PROJECTS,
            MAXIMUM_NUMBER_OF_PROJECTS);

    reportListAs(projectNames, "Projects");

    List<Project> projects = new ArrayList<Project>();
    for(String projectName : projectNames){
        Project aProject = new Project(projectName, projectName);
        projects.add(aProject);
    }

    return projects;
}
```

getProjects and getTodosForProject basically convert a List of String objects into a List
of Project or Todo objects. This means that our shared code randomly generates strings and
we configure the generator with the string templates we want to use.

The main functionality in the get methods is the call to getRandomListFrom method:

```java
projectNames = getRandomListFrom(projectNameSentences,
        MINIMUM_NUMBER_OF_PROJECTS,
        MAXIMUM_NUMBER_OF_PROJECTS);
```

In the above we call getRandomListFrom to define the number of 'things' we want to generate
and the templates that we want to use in the generation.

For:

- Project the template list is projectNameSentences

- Todo the template list is todoNameSentences

Having generated a list of String objects using the template, we write them out to the console for human logging and potential use:

```
reportListAs(projectNames, "Projects");
```

Then convert those String objects into the associated domain object:

```
List<Project> projects = new ArrayList<Project>();
for(String projectName : projectNames){
    Project aProject = new Project(projectName, projectName);
    projects.add(aProject);
}

return projects;
```

We will look at the random list creating in just a second, first I just want to document the output of the list to the console, to get it out of the way:

```
private void reportListAs(List<String> names, String title) {
    System.out.println(title);
    System.out.println("======");

    for(String name : names){
        System.out.println("- " + name + "(" + name +")");
    }
}
```

All this does is iterate over the list of Strings and output them as though they were a list of name/id pairs. So that the user can see what has been created.

Generating a Project Name or TODO

getRandomListFrom

The entry point for generating a name is the getRandomListFrom method.

The parameters to this define the array of sentence templates to use and the number of items to generate.

```
private List<String> getRandomListFrom( String []sentences,
                                        int minimumNumber,
                                        int maximumNumber) {

    List<String> names = new ArrayList<>();

    int numberOfItemsToGenerate =
            r.nextInt(maximumNumber-minimumNumber) +
                    minimumNumber;

    for(int itemNumber = 0;
            itemNumber < numberOfItemsToGenerate; itemNumber++){
        String randomSentenceTemplate =
                sentences[r.nextInt(sentences.length)];
        String randomName =
                buildSentenceFromTemplate(randomSentenceTemplate);
        names.add(randomName);
    }

    return names;
}
```

The key parts of the method are as follows.

First we randomly generate a number in the range to control how many items to generate:

```
int numberOfItemsToGenerate =
        r.nextInt(maximumNumber-minimumNumber) +
                minimumNumber;
```

We iterate for this many items, and for each item, we randomly choose a sentence template to generate from:

```
String randomSentenceTemplate =
        sentences[r.nextInt(sentences.length)];
```

Then we pass the template string into buildSentenceFromTemplate to generate the sentence:

```
String randomName =
              buildSentenceFromTemplate(randomSentenceTemplate);
```

buildSentenceFromTemplate

The buildSentenceFromTemplate method works as follows:

- Use split to create an array of 'terms' in the string that were separated by spaces.
- Iterates over the array processing each 'term' with the getRandomStringFor method.
- All values returned by getRandomStringFor are appended to a string to create a sentence.
- The sentence is returned with trailing spaces removed.

```
private String buildSentenceFromTemplate(String aString){
    String terms[] = aString.split(" ");

    StringBuilder theSentence = new StringBuilder();

    for(String aTerm : terms){
        theSentence.append(getRandomStringFor(aTerm));
        theSentence.append(" ");
    }

    return theSentence.toString().trim();
}
```

getRandomStringFor

The getRandomStringFor method is the interpreter for the 'terms' in the sentence templates.

This matches each term to a Class which implements each term.

Each Class has a method called getItems which will return an Array of String values to select from.

e.g.

- "gv" is replaced by a random value from the strings in the Array returned by the Class GenericVerbs

Hopefully it is obvious from the code below how the other terms map to classes:

```
private String getRandomStringFor(String aTerm) {

    RandomItemsArray itemsArray;

    switch(aTerm){
        case "gv":
            itemsArray = new GenericVerbs();
            break;
        case "fpv":
            itemsArray = new FoodPrepVerbs();
            break;
        case "cfn":
            itemsArray = new CompoundFoodNames();
            break;
        case "cu":
            itemsArray = new CookingUtensils();
            break;
        case "fn":
            itemsArray = new FruitNames();
            break;
        case "vn":
            itemsArray = new VegetableNames();
            break;
        default:
            System.err.println(
                    String.format("You forgot to add %s", aTerm));
            itemsArray = new GenericVerbs();
            break;
    }

    return itemsArray.
            getItems()[r.nextInt(itemsArray.getItems().length)];
}
```

If an invalid 'term' name is used as a parameter then a warning is displayed to the console and the GenericVerbs class is used by default.

The Random Terms Classes

All of the Random Term Classes implement the RandomItemsArray interface and are very similar, so explaining in depth one of them should give you an idea how they work i.e.

GenericVerbs, FoodPrepVerbs, CompoundFoodNames, CookingUtensils, FruitNames, VegetableNames.

The RandomItemsArray interface, mandates the implementation of a single method getItems which returns an array of String objects, from which the data generator randomly selects an item.

```java
public interface RandomItemsArray {
    String[] getItems();
}
```

The classes that implement RandomItemsArray all consist of a hard coded array, and then we return it.

```java
public class GenericVerbs  implements RandomItemsArray {
    public static final String[] items ={
            "buy", "find", "purchase",
            "research the best", "find out what is"
    };

    @Override
    public String[] getItems() {
        return items;
    }
}
```

Summary

This could have been implemented using static text files, since we are randomly selecting an item from the contents.

This might also have made it easier to expand and add new terms, since adding new files is simple and then create a mapping between token and file.

Also this is a very flat generator. It isn't possible in its current form for a 'term' in the sentence to be implemented of other 'terms' which would make the generation more flexible.

In retrospect:

- This is a very simple approach.

- It was fast to create for the specific code.
- It isn't very flexible.
- In order to expand we have to change the code.

For a more flexible example of a very similar approach I will suggest looking at the Test Data Generator that I wrote for my "Evil Tester Sloganizer" in JavaScript.

The Sloganizer generator is text based - although the data is still hard coded, and does support recursive term expansion.

You can find:

- description of the sloganizer on my blog,
    - blog.eviltester.com/2016/09/how-to-write-simple-random-test-data.html[165]
- the code for the sloganizer on GitHub,
    - github.com/eviltester/sloganizer[166]

---

[165] http://blog.eviltester.com/2016/09/how-to-write-simple-random-test-data.html
[166] https://github.com/eviltester/sloganizer

Appendix - Other REST GUI Clients

Postman[167] is not the only REST GUI client.

But it is the one that I use most often.

I have also used Paw[168] on the Mac.

This list is to provide you with alternatives should you wish to evaluate other tools for your workflow.

I can't guarantee that the list below is up to date, or even if the tools listed still exist.

Fortunately, lists of lists, which are updated and maintained do exist, e.g. more clients are listed on the 'awesome-rest list':

- github.com/marmelab/awesome-rest[169]

Chrome Applications

Chrome are removing support for Chrome Applications, so the following may either fade into the ether or, like Postman, morph into Desktop Applications.

- Insomnia[170]
- Advanced REST Client[171]
- DHC REST Client[172]
- Postman[173]

---

[167] https://www.getpostman.com/
[168] https://luckymarmot.com/paw
[169] https://github.com/marmelab/awesome-rest#testing
[170] http://insomnia.rest/
[171] https://chromerestclient.appspot.com/
[172] https://chrome.google.com/webstore/detail/dhc-rest-client/aejoelaoggembcahagimdiliamlcdmfm
[173] https://www.getpostman.com/

Desktop Applications

- Insomnia[174]
- Postman[175]

Mac Only

- Cocoa Rest Client[176]

Not Free & Mac only

- Paw[177]

Firefox Plugin

- REST Client[178] and the official page[179]

IDE and Editor Plugins

IntelliJ Plugin

- IntelliJ REST Client[180]

Atom Text Editor Plugin

- Rest Client Package[181]

---

[174]http://insomnia.rest/
[175]https://www.getpostman.com/
[176]http://mmattozzi.github.io/cocoa-rest-client/
[177]https://luckymarmot.com/paw
[178]https://addons.mozilla.org/en-GB/firefox/addon/restclient/
[179]http://restclient.net/
[180]https://www.jetbrains.com/help/idea/2016.1/rest-client-tool-window.html
[181]https://atom.io/packages/rest-client

Appendix - HTTP Debug Proxy and Proxy Support Tools

Throughout the book I mention HTTP proxies.

I tend to use HTTP Proxies a lot, after having sent a message to the API, either from cURL, Postman or my automated abstractions.

If you don't already use Proxies then I highly recommend you start. Your visibility into the workings of your application will increase dramatically. And you instantly have a lot more options in how you can interact with the system.

You can find information about all the Proxies and support tools from the following websites:

- HTTP Debug Proxies
    - Fiddler[182] (Windows Only)
    - OWasp Zap[183]
    - BurpSuite[184]
    - Charles[185]
- Proxy Support Tools
    - FoxyProxy Standard
        * Firefox Plugin[186]
        * Chrome Plugin[187]

---

[182] http://www.telerik.com/fiddler

[183] https://www.owasp.org/index.php/OWASP_Zed_Attack_Proxy_Project

[184] https://portswigger.net/burp/

[185] https://www.charlesproxy.com/

[186] https://addons.mozilla.org/en-US/firefox/addon/foxyproxy-standard/

[187] https://chrome.google.com/webstore/detail/foxyproxy-standard/gcknhkkoolaabfmlnjonogaaifnjlfnp

Appendix - Creating Random Data for Tracks v 2.2.0 Testing

When working on a workshop for Tracks v2.2.0 I took a different approach for generating data for the Tracks Application.

Approach

Wunderlist.com[188] is a popular TODO list manager, and at one point had a page with a set of example Projects and TODO items from those Projects.

To save time, I decided to:

- Scrape that data from the page.
- Store the data in a cache.

Then to create data in the Tracks system I iterated over these Project names and TODOs and added them as data in the Tracks system.

This has the following drawbacks:

- The data is probably copyright Wunderlist and can't really be published.
- The data may contain invalid characters that don't work in Tracks.
- The data might not be appropriate and might need to be sanitised.

Because of copyright, I haven't distributed actual Wunderlist data in the source code.

I have create example files that have the same format as the Wunderlist files but have entirely different data.

You can find the example cache files in:

---

[188] http://wunderlist.com

- `src\test\resources\version_2_2_0_data`

The files are:

- `wunderlistProjects.properties`
- `wunderlistTodos.properties`

The good thing about using data from the site was that I had about 2000-3000 Task names that were pretty unique and about 200 Project names. I have cut down the above files considerably.

Scraping Data Support Classes

The code to scrape the data from the Wunderlist site is in:

- `src\main\java`
- `package api.version_2_2_0.wunderlist.appasapi;`

The main classes to support this are:

- `WunderlistCache` which contains all the code to read property files containing data scraped from the site and loads them into memory as `List` of `Project` and `Todo` objects.
- `Project` and `Todo` are simple data classes representing the domain objects
- `Wunderlist` is the class that contains the code for scraping the web page.

Since the `Wunderlist` class uses REST Assured in a slightly different way than the code in version 2.3.0, I will explore this in a little more detail.

Scraping Data Code

The scraping code:

- Uses REST Assured to issue a `GET` on the URL containing the data.
- Extracts the HTML from the `body` of the request.
- Uses a REGEX to parse the data from the page.
- Converts the data into a `List` of `Project` objects.

```java
public List<Project> getPublicProjects(){

    String aUrl = "https://wunderlist.com/discover";
    Response projectsHtml = when().get(aUrl).
                            then().extract().response();

    String projectListHtml = projectsHtml.body().asString();

    String titlepattern = "<div class=\"editors-card\" title=\"([^\"]*)\">";
    String urlpattern = "<a href=\"/list/(\\d*)\">";
    Pattern p = Pattern.compile(titlepattern + "\\s*" + urlpattern);
    Matcher m = p.matcher(projectListHtml);

    List<Project> projects = new ArrayList<Project>();

    System.out.println("Projects");
    System.out.println("======");

    while( m.find()){

        String titlegroupy = m.group(1);
        String urlgroupy = m.group(2);
        System.out.println("- " + titlegroupy + "(" + urlgroupy +")");
        Project aProject = new Project(titlegroupy, urlgroupy);
        projects.add(aProject);
    }


    return projects;
}
```

The GET call uses a simple REST Assured call, and doesn't require a given section since there are no headers to configure, so we can simply issue a GET on a desired URL.

```java
String aUrl = "https://wunderlist.com/discover";
Response projectsHtml = when().get(aUrl).
                        then().extract().response();
```

Also note that then().extract().response() is used to return the Response.

We use the Response object to convert the body to a String. The body will contain the full HTML page "<html>...</html>".

```java
String projectListHtml = projectsHtml.body().asString();
```

Rather than use an HTML parser on the page, it seemed simpler to use a REGEX to parse the page and extract the data.

It didn't really matter if it wasn't a proper HTML parser, so long as we managed to get text data into the `Project` details.

The REGEX parsing using straight Java:

```java
String titlepattern = "<div class=\"editors-card\" title=\"([^\"]*)\">";
String urlpattern = "<a href=\"/list/(\\d*)\">";
Pattern p = Pattern.compile(titlepattern + "\\s*" + urlpattern);
Matcher m = p.matcher(projectListHtml);
```

`Pattern.compile` is used to create a REGEX pattern then we use the `matcher` method to apply it to the HTML page returned.

The code then iterates over the items that match the pattern by using the `find` method to find the next matching string.

```java
while( m.find()){

    String titlegroupy = m.group(1);
    String urlgroupy = m.group(2);
    System.out.println("- " + titlegroupy + "(" + urlgroupy +")");
    Project aProject = new Project(titlegroupy, urlgroupy);
    projects.add(aProject);
}
```

For each match, the `group` method is used to retrieve the data from the REGEX match.

The code to get and parse the TODOs is so similar that I don't see any value in describing it here. You can read it in the code.

You can find more details on Java REGEX parsing on-line:

- Offical documentation on Regular Expressions
    - docs.oracle.com/javase/tutorial/essential/regex/[189]
- Offical documentation on Pattern
    - docs.oracle.com/javase/8/docs/api/java/util/regex/Pattern.html[190]

---

[189]https://docs.oracle.com/javase/tutorial/essential/regex/
[190]https://docs.oracle.com/javase/8/docs/api/java/util/regex/Pattern.html

Testing the Utility `@Test` Class

To build up the Utility `@Test` Classes, I created a set of 'helper' `@Test` methods which let me check that each part of my process worked.

You can find my code in:

- `src\test\java`
- `package api.version_2_2_0.appasapi.wunderlist`

The `WunderListAppAsApiTest` contains four `@Test` methods. The class has been annotated `@Ignore` because they no longer work with the changes to Wunderlist.com.

The four `@Test` methods are:

- `canRetrievePublicProjectList`
- `canRetrieveTodoForProjectList`
- `canCachePublicProjectList`
- `canCachePublicProjectTodoList`

I would run this class prior to running the utility `@Test` which creates the data in Tracks because if any of these tests fail then I know that I can't retrieve the information from Wunderlist or read and write to the cache files.

These four `@Test` methods exercise the `WunderlistCache` and `Wunderlist` classes.

Setup Data with the Utility `@Test` Class

I won't describe the `SetupTracksTestDataTest` class in detail, you can find the code in:

- `package api.version_2_2_0.trackstestdata;`

The code was hacked together and hasn't been refactored at all.

When you examine the code you'll see commented out configuration from previous execution.

I have one `@Test` called `updateWunderlistCache` which does exactly that - it scrapes the data from Wunderlist and adds it to the cache.

The other `@Test` called `createTracksDataFromWunderlistCache`:

- Reads the information from the cache.
- Creates users in the system using the Tracks "App as API".
- Adds Projects from the cache - making them unique by adding a 'random word' to each Project.
- Adds TODOs from the cache, again appending a 'random word' to make them unique.

The 'random word' uses an early version of the simple random word generation code that you saw earlier:

```java
private String randomWord() {
    return String.valueOf(System.currentTimeMillis()).
                            replaceAll("1", "a").
                            replaceAll("2", "d").
                            replaceAll("3", "o").
                            replaceAll("4", "n").
                            replaceAll("5", "e").
                            replaceAll("6", "r").
                            replaceAll("7", "h").
                            replaceAll("8", "i").
                            replaceAll("9", "t").
                            replaceAll("0", "s");
}
```

Exploring Tracks API with Postman REST Client

Postman is free and is available as a Chrome Application.

- getpostman.com[191]

Essentially a standalone Chrome plugin.

The Postman GUI is simple to use.

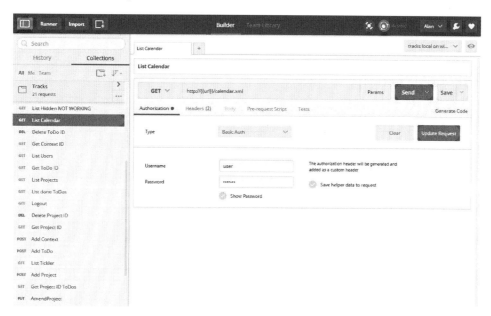

Postman GUI

- Central part of the screen is where we issue requests
- Left hand side bar is a set of 'collections' of saved requests

---

[191]https://www.getpostman.com/

Postman will 'sync' collections of requests to all devices, I find this useful since I often switch between working on the Windows machine, and on a Mac, and Postman will sync the changes I made to the collection on one machine with the other so I always have an up to date set of messages to use.

The Postman Chrome Application has much the same functionality as the Desktop Application. The main differences are found when working through a Proxy.

Using Postman Through a Proxy

Postman will pick up your Chrome browser settings so if you have Chrome going through a proxy then Postman will also go through a proxy.

Shared Cookie Jar Gotcha

Because Postman is a Chrome Application it will share the same cookie jar as Chrome.

This can be helpful if you want to issue requests after logging in via the GUI, but if you are trying to test the API separate from the GUI it can sometimes cause sessions to bleed over.

On a previous version of Tracks I lost about 2 hours investigating a defect where a user could access anyone's account. But in reality, I was logged in to the GUI as Admin in Chrome and my session was being shared by the 'normal' user in the Postman REST Client.

About the Author

Alan Richardson has more than twenty years of professional IT experience, working as a programmer, and at every level of the testing hierarchy from Tester through Head of Testing. Author of the books "Dear Evil Tester", "Selenium Simplified" and "Java For Testers". Alan has also created on-line training courses to help people learn Technical Web Testing and Selenium WebDriver with Java.

Alan works as an independent consultant, helping companies improve their automating and use of agile, and exploratory technical testing.

You can find Alan's writing and training videos on:

- SeleniumSimplified.com[192],
- EvilTester.com[193],
- JavaForTesters.com[194], and
- CompendiumDev.co.uk[195].

Alan posts information and videos regularly to social media on:

- Twitter - @eviltester[196]
- Instagram - @eviltester[197]
- Linkedin - @eviltester[198]
- Youtube - EvilTesterVideos[199]
- Pinterest - @eviltester[200]

To contact Alan for custom training or consultancy, visit:

- compendiumdev.co.uk/contact[201]

---

[192] http://SeleniumSimplified.com
[193] http://EvilTester.com
[194] http://javafortesters.com
[195] http://compendiumdev.co.uk
[196] https://twitter.com/eviltester
[197] https://www.instagram.com/eviltester
[198] https://uk.linkedin.com/in/eviltester
[199] https://www.youtube.com/user/EviltesterVideos
[200] https://uk.pinterest.com/eviltester/
[201] http://compendiumdev.co.uk/page/contact_us

Printed in Great Britain
by Amazon